CHIPS

DAVE DELAPP

Dave DeLapp – Chips

First Edition 2017

International Standard Book Number
Trade paperback: 978-0-9830292-6-7

Design and production:
Cohographics, Salem Oregon
cohographics.com

Printed in the U.S.A.
Gorham Printing, Centralia Washington
gorhamprinting.com

Cover art: Paul Toews

Dave DeLapp
P.O. Box 483
Lyons, OR 97358
503-859-3277

DEDICATION

In dedication of my book I have to say that my sister Jean put the real pressure on me to write down my thoughts. She had a couple items published in national magazines and when reading what I submitted to her, she said, "Chip, you should put these thoughts in writing." So it was with her encouragement that I decided at least two of us thought it was worth my time. I only wish that she had lived till now to review these things that I have recalled, but there are lots of things we wait too long to do.

ABOUT THE AUTHOR

Nicknamed "Chip" by next-door neighbor "Old Granny Renner," David was born on October 15, 1928—the last of the DeLapp lineage. His father, Bud DeLapp, had moved with his wife and two small offspring from Illinois to Salem in 1914. After relocating several times over the next five years, he finally bought a sixteen-acre farm in Eola with a big two story, framed, unplumbed house and settled in with his family and mother, with a steady job paying $25 for a six day week. Demonstrating thrift by milking a cow, raising a garden, keeping pigs and laying hens, he worked a miracle providing well for the family. As a school board member the DeLapps became the foundation of community involvement.

With the unfortunate event of the ultimate house warming one cold Sunday morning in January, the old house with all belongings burnt clear to the ground. The next day the whole neighborhood started clearing away the debris and constructing a new temporary housing which the family lived in for two years during the rebuilding. This seeming catastrophe proved to be lemonade out of lemons, with rebuilding a new fourbedroom home with indoor plumbing and a basement with furnace, made possible with an FHA loan at $36 a month.

Mom later said, "If I had known it was going to turn out this way, I would have burned it down a long time ago." With this character inheritance, Chip grew up without preaching but always reaching for the higher rung. With setups and setbacks for 86 years, there was always another spring.

CONTENTS

1

COMING OUT OF THE STARTING GATE

WEST SALEM AND ME

This is where it all began for me. Mom and Dad had settled in this big old two-story house on 16 acres in the Eola school district, four miles west of Salem. On October 15, 1928 through luck, the family improved immeasurably, even with

THE AUTHOR

kids already better than average. Ethel, Sammy and Beth were pretty. Bub and Babe were healthy. Dump was fat and cute but they must have known perfection hadn't been obtained until Chip came along because Dad took one look and said, "That's it!"

We lived in the old two-story frame house with no foundation and an unfinished upstairs (cold) and unfinished outhouse (cold), until one Sunday morning Mom gave it the ultimate remodel job (hot). Barefoot and in pajamas, I shivered in Renner's house next door and watched 300-foot flames inaugurate a new beginning and building project. That building project was a new fourbedroom house built in 1936 with the new FHA loan that was $6,000 at 6% interest, with a payment of $36 a month.

So from the disaster of a burning down house and burning up everything we owned came the new era of a new house, indoor plumbing, four-bedrooms, and a wood burning furnace—a comfort we had never experienced before. During these two years of construction we lived in a one-bedroom house that the neighbors had come and built in a day. There were five kids at home and my mother and dad which wasn't enough, so we had a hired man, George Hall, living with us who slept in the hay loft in the barn. It was up to Bub and George Hall and a horse with a slip scraper to dig the basement for the new house. Of course at the same time we had to go to school, take care of the animals and the berry fields and everything else of normal everyday life. What depression? The goals were there, the opportunities beyond imagination.

PHASE ONE OF A LIFE LEGACY
3080 Lancaster

To recapture the memory of home don't we all revert to our youth? The days of just growing up without cares, without planning, with just being ourselves. I was lucky having parents who did all the worrying, working and planning. They were good parents, and they made a home that formed our character and our lives which in turn gave us the built-in life achievement of being able to create a home feeling for our progeny. If the other kids had bad parents, you could see it on their faces. We were happy.

I can separate my life into very distinct phases and the first 16 years I look back on as home. My mother and father followed the natural conception program accepted in the first 18 years of marriage in that era of having a baby every two years until I was born.

Also, it was 1928 and a year later the Depression hit and seven kids were enough to care for. A happy home? Maybe being the youngest added significance, but growing up, being fed, sleeping warm, playing games, and going to a small school of only 23 kids, what was not to be happy about? A little farm with a cow, sheep, chickens, horse, dogs and cats; sure they had to be cared for, but who thought about these chores as being work? They had to be done and everybody did them. This was during the '30s and we, like everyone else, were contented to create within the home environment our own fun. The Depression Era, I think, was the best few years of creative entertainment that we've had in 100 years. Radio, Chinese checkers, Monopoly, card parties, community monthly socials at the school, coasting down the hill on wagons and bikes, swimming in the river in our own "private swimming pool," playing in the basement.

All these nostalgic pasts of growing up I don't think have ever been reproduced. I have reflected on how and where my kids have considered to be their home place, and I think—unconsciously—I may have effectively recreated my childhood home in buying a small farm on Lancaster Drive, Salem, in similar environments to what I grew up in.

MARTEL — ANCESTORS OF CHARLEMAGNE —
1,200 YEARS LATER

THE FUTURE BEGINS

A whole full-length movie could be made about the 16 acre West Salem farm and the berry fields:

The whole house burning down. The neighbors coming and building a new house in a day so the family could stay together. It was a one-bedroom 24×36 house, just framed in, no finished inside walls, but with a floor and bedrooms. We lived there for two years.

Making a team of horses with the neighbor's old Duke and our old Buster to work both farms. Buster was a monument to the animal world: Used, abused, petted, rode, but always fed and through it all still as individual as any horse ever born. He didn't like to have his afternoons interrupted in the pasture. Go up and get old Buster and work that ground—sure, just try to catch that old bastard in an open field.

Bob, the collie, got old and died here and Jerry, the pup, started his life here and lived it to the fullest. Neighbor Renners, John and Willow, cousins, aunts and uncles; what a book that would be! This termed our first 16 years. So many more events of major unimportance with relative importance occurred in our growing up there that we must write the whole story of cows, goats, sheep, ducks, turkeys, berries, cherries, prunes, nuts, garden, rock garden, picket fence, putting in wood, going swimming.

On to the next plateau: the Gervais flats. I always knew those Sunday farm lookings would get us into trouble. What a challenge! Same problems only magnified. More land, more horses, more cows, more turkeys, more work, another remodeling job. The big war ending, everyone home safe—and when Babe took one look at that buried John Deere tractor in the mud, he was ready to go back. It was wet, but home. And farming was the living, not a hobby. Dad finally quit Price's, and took up Pinochle playing full time, and grandkids all knew Grampy and Grammy's farm. And Leon, the wayward nephew, showed up with ice and ripe bananas.

I thought I had that farm looking good when I went to Korea. But they just couldn't do it without me so they sold it, and I came back to the 160 acres in Colton. Is this the start of the second book? Another dairy, clearing out, building a hog barn, breaking a leg, married, first little house, remodeled log house and everyone married and hitting their stride. Having kids, getting ahead and Leon still showing up with ice and ripe bananas.

Trading farms for two houses and money, I witnessed the real estate business and bought my first place at Scott's Mills. I had three kids, Dump had her two, Babe had his two, Bub stopped at four, Beth—three little girls, Sammy had four mixed, and even Ethel got into the mother act with one. So with this, I'll end this resumé with all out of the nest, not scattered too far.

We still get together and eat food by the ton, but we still have these unanswered questions. Why did we have an address at 135 Liberty when we lived four miles out of town? Why did cousin Bill Hoyt get poison oak and never had to work on our farm, and none of us could get it even if we drank a quart of it. Why didn't we own a good boat? Why didn't I have a pony? Why didn't we keep that old Model T pickup? Why is Bub left handed? And is Babe's fixation on milking cows (pulling tits) really normal?

All these nostalgic pasts of growing up I don't think have ever been reproduced. I have tried to reproduce for my kids the feeling of growing up in the old home place with the worry free environment that I had experienced as a child.

THE BERRY BUSINESS

I was just one-year old when October 1929 came. I don't think I started the depression as a whole, but I probably depressed mom and daddy. But anyway, after the bright idea to not give me a gunny sack swimming lesson, they conceived of the idea of raising loganberries. I don't know where that idea came from, but it had all the fragrance of mom. And looking back at how hard she worked at it, and suffered without complaint, I have a suspicion she had quite a bit of input in the venture. Can't you hear her, "Why shoot, I and the kids can train those vines and hoe those weeds and pick most of 'em, and berries will always sell." (We know that's how fortunes are made and asses are lost. Thank God they stopped trying to make their own labor force).

When one considers all the cedar pots, all the wire, all the holes to dig, plants to to buy, ground to work—with no tractor, just Fred the horse (who got infection and had to be shot)—the question comes up: What the hell were they thinking of? Why loganberries? At 2 and ½ cents a pound, we grossed $250 on 5 tons of berries (about 675 crates). It cost $67.50 to pick them at 10¢ a crate. Of course we probably picked 75 crates, so we paid $60 to outside help; this leaves $190 to plow, work, hoe, train, put back vines, tear old vines off—all year long—and this includes fighting, threatening, sunburn, ice cream, cold pop, and gasoline. God tried to tell us something when the oldest patch got diseased and we had to take them out. It should have happened to them all. I don't know at what time, or what happening occurred that the decision was made it wasn't paying, but it wasn't soon enough. The three rows of Himalaya blackberries stayed (they're still trying to kill those damned things off), and we made a little on them selling to the winery (that's where we should have sold the logans).

Character building? Sure, right along there with horse whipping and slavery, but we did make some pretty good loganberry wine.

BUCK

For some unknown reason when I was a kid we had a gender problem in naming the animals. The female duck was Bill, the spayed female cat was Tojo and my pretty ewe lamb was Buck. I can justify the name somewhat by her lamb-like antics and gyrations that we called a 'buck jump' of a Spring lamb on a warm Spring day.

She was given to me as a 4-H lamb project in the old lamb project, started by a couple who moved into the community with one boy, Lauren. They gave him anything he wanted, so they were leaders of the Lamb Club and brought five bummer lambs from a friend's ranch in eastern Oregon, giving each one of us a nice lamb for free. While Lauren and I made pets of ours, the visions of lamb chops predominated the thinking of the other depression era three. We had a cow with lots of milk, so Buck got her four bottle-feedings a day. Being warmed in the kitchen of our new house, it was no time at all until come feeding time, and three hops up the steps there was a lamb in the kitchen with no complaints from my mother, who was the same woman who brought in sixteen piglets to keep them warm under the gas range.

With twice as much milk, plus flower tips, rosebuds, and garden sprouts, Buck grew twice as fast as the other lambs in the club. I also had the advantage of our next door neighbor, Ronald Hogg, being a nationally recognized sheep breeder and judge, who would stop by and give me tips on hoof trimming and finally show fitting. Buck took blue ribbons at the county fair, so come state fair, we were ready to go. Buck didn't like the confinement and crowds at the fair, so she was soon identified as that sheep that kept jumping out her pen and running all over the stock barn. In showing Buck, I ran into one small problem: there was no classification for her, not being a registered purebred. So she ended up being the only lamb in Oregon State Fair history taking First Prize by a ewe raised in the Willamette Valley of the Eastern Oregon Cross-bred Ram category. I won $12.

She was the foundation of the herd. We bought the other four members, which were all ewes, and had five, all of which produced lambs, and Buck sheared a beautiful wool fleece of 22 pounds, with the average being 10–12. We had to sell her and the others when we sold the farm.

BUB'S DRIVING LESSON

We all know we don't always plan our good fortune; most times it's a "right time, right place" happening. Such a happening was my first driving lesson given by brother Bub. The never-forgotten elements of a Model-T, berry field, hot day, and yellow jackets make up this story. Bub fixed up and started driving the $10 Model-T when they were both illegal, which started his lifetime history of automobile mechanics. At the time of the incident, he was probably 15 and I was nine years old. We all knew that Bub swelled up like a poisoned pup when stung by bees. He was, and still is, very aware (hysterical) of a bee. The action started that day when he stopped the pickup on a yellow jacket's nest while unloading berry crates, halfway up the row of our Loganberry patch.

Although some world records are made, some are never recognized; for example, who would ever believe a 9-year-old who had witnessed his older brother run the 100-yard dash in less than 9 seconds? I was just coming into the berry patch when here streaks my big brother. It was only after he had put considerable distance between him and the bees (no bee could fly as fast as he was travelling) that he stopped where I was.

So here occurs the right time and place for my first big experience. I was old enough to know he wasn't going back to get that Model-T. He had left the engine running, so he knew I could handle it in an open field. So, with much big brotherly assurance, and a 25 cent bribe, he convinced me I could sneak back to the 'T' unnoticed by the bees, climb in, push the pedal down, and drive it "by myself"—and I did it! I always believed Bub. If Bub said, I could do it, I could do it. It has always been so.

MARY ALICE ELLIOT

I t was while I was reading a book a couple of weeks ago that I had this revelation about something that happened to me 30 years ago. The book I'm reading is about a girl who was born and raised in a concentration camp in North Korea and the degradation that she endured in the horrible circumstances that she saw. Death was her only salvation. Then a woman came to the camp and picked her out of several hundred to take her with her and make a life for her. It was while I was reading this that it suddenly occurred to me how important such a thing could be to that person.

Years ago, when I was in grade school, we had a poor family with four girls living in the community during the middle of depression. My mother invited one of them home with us to have dinner, stay all night, and she was given a bath-dinner, clean clothes, etc.

One morning a few years ago, a woman called me at my office after having seen my name in my advertising and asked if I went to Eola School. I said yes, and she told me that 30 years ago, my mother had invited her to our home. "You will never know how much that meant to me," she said, "because at that time, I realized life could be better." When this author made such an extreme example out of the degradation of torture that some people have endured, the simple act of human kindness takes on a significance and can affect someone deeply, as it did in Mary Elliott's life-changing experience.

Mom

M uch can be attributed to my mother, who was a member of the Willing Workers class at the Salem First Christian Church and always helped with the school socials and paid a lot of attention to the kids we brought home. She would give them a bath, clean them up and give them freshly washed clothes. Dad was the type of person who did a good job providing, and always had the attitude that one more plate at the table didn't matter. Once, there was a little boy that had been abandoned so mom took him in, but there was no place to sleep in the house, so he slept in the bed with Beth. He crawled right up and crapped in Beth's hair that night. Beth later married, and as her gift from God she had three girls.

EOLA SCHOOL AND EDNA GRANT

For some reason, after I started grade school, the teachers at my school only lasted two years, so from grade one to eight I had four teachers. The teacher for the first and second grade was Edna Grant. Now, Edna had been there five years before I, so two more years was all she could take. I don't know for a fact that I had anything to do with this, but it does seem con-sequential that after two years I had a new teacher.

Edna Grant was young and plainly pretty with no makeup. At that time, a seven year longevity indicated she was approved by the community. The school building was a one-room, very close, no draft building, heated by a wood furnace in the rear, with no ventilation to preserve warmth,

TERRIBLE TWENTY

and accommodating 35 kids grade one to eight. Edna had a good handle on discipline with country kids and, with the school board permission, she exacted this discipline with a short rubber hose about five feet long, which she administered quite effectively.

But one situation arose that this demure, polite, little woman had trouble with. This was during the depression era when for a lot of households the diet consisted of beans. Well, 35 kids passing gas in a confined schoolroom was more than Edna could handle. So, she, with all the decorum and modesty she could generate, announced one morning

that when the biological function of having to pass gas occurred, the student would be excused from the room and had to go outside and stand on the little hill. There was a lumber mill towards the coast, named *Fort Hill*. It didn't take long to name this mound. A procedure never adopted by the school district, but it worked for Edna.

THREE OF TWENTY

It's Only a Game

I n 1936 a family game swept the nation: Monopoly. A masterpiece of timing, the game brought a fantasy to those times of economic depression. A money game of buying and selling real estate where your future was determined by the toss of the dice and how well you invested. To the family with no chance for a real world wheeling and dealing, this provided the perfect escape. Our family was no exception. We were a large family working hard on a berry farm, our dad working in town, and dreaming of a bigger farm, more income, the good life. Who in that family would have dreamed that a money game, with a name we didn't know the meaning of, would affect the youngest—me—with such vital force?

The game was made for me. I lived, breathed, dreamed, and gloried in the game. At nine years old, I had every rent on every property memorized, knew the odds of landing on each one, figured comparative values, and much to the annoyance of my older brothers and sisters, continually patted my money to keep it all neat and tidy. The thrill of collecting rent has stayed with me, buying the little green houses and building motels was a joy inexpressible. It was my character builder.

My family was able to buy that bigger farm. My brother was a farmer with farmer dedication. I farmed with him for 15 years but truly was never a farmer. When marriage dictated a choosing of professions, I, by accident (or subconscious design), got into the real estate selling profession. I immediately knew the comfort, and at the same time the excitement I felt when playing monopoly in the basement when I was nine years old.

I have been in this business a long time. In looking around me, very few that started with me are still around. I've built the houses on Pennsylvania Avenue; I've collected rent from Broadway and Park Place; and I've been sent back before passing Go. Many people have profound happenings that they look back on to have influenced their lives. Many people don't know what the influence was or why they developed the way they did. Probably very few can look back and see the effect as clearly as I can. It all began with playing Monopoly.

DAD'S HIDDEN SURPRISE

Dad worked as a shoe salesman and had his little fresh farm produce business on the side, in which he bartered for groceries to a large market in Salem. Blackberry season was our best, and for 6 weeks we ate high on the hog.

After one particularly good morning delivery, he brought home that evening a whole stalk of bananas, and to keep them from ripening too fast (and hide them from us) he hung them in his bedroom closet. Well, to a bunch of farm kids, a banana in those days was a treat better than candy, so when we located the cache, we felt some entitlement because we had picked the berries—the orgy was on. Grandma loved bananas, Mom had a couple, and us kids sneaked them out all day long and even let the neighbor boy help himself. So it came as little surprise to us, when dad came home and slipped into the closet to get himself a banana, that he came back to the kitchen carrying just the stalk. "Every damn one is gone," is all he could say in stark disbelief. Needless to say, he was the only one to appreciate Mom's banana cream pie for dessert.

SCRAMBLED EGGS AT FITTS MARKET

When I was a boy in 1938, and Salem was a small town

During the 30's depression Dad sold shoes at Oscar Price's Shoe Store and also had a little side business of farm raised products which included fresh eggs sold to Fitts Market on Commercial Street in downtown Salem. Dad delivered on his way to work, so he was always dressed in a suit and tie. On this particular morning, as he unloaded the heavily laden crate, the bottom completely gave way and dropped 30 dozen fresh eggs on the sidewalk. Ira Fitts came out of his store and there was my father standing dressed up, ankle deep in broken eggs. At one look all Ira could do was to start laughing and all Dad could do was join him. So here were two grown men in a pile of eggs with tears of laughter and all Ira could say was, "Bud, it looks like tomorrow I'll have to advertise fresh eggs already scrambled."

Bud DeLapp retired after 38 years at Price's. Fitts Market is still in business on 12th Street.

JERRY

Our neighbor, who trained dogs as a hobby, told my dad when I was very young that "in your lifetime you will be lucky to have that one special dog." Sixty-five years and many dogs later, I know he was right. Jerry was that dog. Everyone who has ever owned a dog is sure they have the smartest animal that has ever lived. I have had some smart dogs, but I have often wished my kids had half the smarts and personality as Jerry.

First of all, you've got to understand dogs. Jerry wasn't a mongrel who got lucky having brains—he was a livestock dog with breeding of intelligence. A border collie's sensitivity and an Australian shepherd's guts and class. He was beautifully marked with the breed's mottled gray and distinctive white eye. He had class. A furry ball of a pup, who would heel a calf or pig with the natural inborn instinct from the time he was weaned. I believe playing was his whole persona. Everything he did was with verve, fortitude, and every move an expression of a joy in living. He became another kid in our family of seven and perhaps may have even taken on a family personality just by his growing up with us. His training by us was no more a conscious instruction than any of the rest of us kids got.

His first inauguration to life on our farm was by Buster, the work horse. When Jerry heeled him the first time, Buster very forcefully and accurately kicked him like a furry football a good 20 feet. That really proved to be the wrong move for that horse as he found out until the day he died. With that last heel to go through the barn door he got very forcefully nipped. Jerry never forgot, he just learned to nip and duck.

A stock dog has many jobs but usually with a type of livestock that suits him. A cattle dog must be aggressive, a sheep dog must herd, Jerry had to do it all. Our family farm had pigs, ducks, chickens, turkeys, cows, calves, a horse, and all needed to be handled differently. One minute Jerry could make an ornery bull get into his pen and the next minute nudge a baby pig through a hole in the fence with his nose. As soon as he was big enough one of the duties that Jerry had to perform was bringing the cows from the pasture to the barn. We only had two or three or four but our farm laid long and narrow, so for the cows to go to pasture they had a walk up this long lane to where the pasture was, out of sight of the house.

This farm was also on three elevations, so the back part was up to the third elevation where we couldn't see them. When the grass was high they didn't want to come to the barn in the evenings, which they normally would do just to get feed, so we would say, "Jerry get-way-by, bring the cows," and he would take up that lane like a streak of lightning out of sight, and maybe as many as 30 minutes later he would come with the cows and the horse, whatever was ours, down to the gate, to put them in the barn.

Our neighbor also pastured the same land we did. They had a couple milk cows, and the neighbor adamantly verified that when Jerry brought the animals down to the 'Y,' Jerry separated them and brought ours to our gate, and theirs went to their barn. The only reason we can believe this is that we never once had one of their cows come down our lane.

It was all play, and me being eight years old when we got him, I also liked to play. Who could field a hard-hit ground ball without a miss center field? Jerry. He would play ball for hours, catching and running with it and then dropping it at my feet to throw or hit again. My new football had him stumped.

He would run it down and cradle it between front paws, but this fooled him until he discovered he could slide his tooth under the lacing. Then he became a football player. As one of the family he always went with us on our annual one-week vacation. The coast or mountains, there were waves to jump or squirrels to chase or big dogs to challenge—he made it all fun.

Dad was a member of the school board for several years. One of the other members was Ernie Brunk who had two ornery boys about six and eight years old. One evening he came to see dad about a school meeting and brought the two boys with him. So after being in the house for quite a while he said, well, I better go out and see what trouble those two boys are into. When he went out he was very surprised to see the two boys sitting in the back-seat with Jerry lying outside, eyeing both of them. When asked, the oldest one said, we threw a rock at the dog and Jerry very promptly put them back in the car and stood there. Dad always said it was the only time those kids ever had a discipline, and it had to be my dog that did it.

Jerry's love of life also had a life of love. If a female friend was in heat miles away, we couldn't keep him home. Everyone knew who the father was to all those white eyed pups in the hills.

We believe Jerry going missing was due to a stock buyer watching him herd our sow and 12 pigs off the highway one day, walking them down the shoulder and bringing them back home. The next day Jerry was gone. Efforts by us and the sheriffs and state police never ever found him. No other dog has ever taken his place. The six years as part of our family was as real and joyful as anyone could have. We all can remember that cocked ear and that white eye, and that energy that says, "Aren't we having fun?"

FRENCH PRAIRIE SAGA

1

I n the spring of 1945, on one rainy Sunday afternoon, we took a "go look at a farm" tour. Dad had let it be known in Salem that he wanted a farm; why he wanted a farm never was established, but I think it was something like "I never owned a fire truck, but I'd like to." With written directions we drove something like 40 miles of gravel road to finally spot this Big Red Barn, sitting like Noah's Ark in a sea of water and mud, on Keene Road, Gervais.

We must establish first the fact that the Gervais-St. Louis area was flat, and by that I mean water—two inches deep—covering miles and miles of ground. The only elevation in a radius of 20 miles from this farm was the S.P. & S. Railroad that ran right through the middle of the prairie land we were considering. Railroad frontage actually has little advantageas to farming and several disadvantages, which we were to find out. But we had found it—exactly what we had been searching for.

We learned later that this was *The Old Ben Hall Farm*, and well, *Old Ben Hall* was one of the old boys who had built a nice barn, but the house and outbuildings were bonfires needing lit. Ben had died and his widow was letting her sister and husband and son Delbert Shellito (whose lamp was low on kerosene) and his wife rent the farm.

The deal we made was lock, stock and barrel: 15 milk cows, some skinny calves, a sow and pigs, four horses, and all machinery, plus 110 acres with a good barn, 3-bedroom house, plus the outbuildings and A WORKING WATER PUMPING WINDMILL!! What a deal! Well, Dad could hardly wait until Monday to make his offer of $12,000 cash on closing—take it or leave it. And surprise, surprise! They took it. Can you imagine how many times that following week that he woke up saying, "Now what have I done?"

2

Mom was never in doubt. She was checking the price of turkey poults the day the deal was accepted. The week after our first inspection we rushed back out there to look again and we couldn't find the place. Dad laughed and said, "We'll have to stop and ask the neighbors where the farm, that those people from Salem bought, is." On our second inspection we also learned that included with the equipment was a 1928 GMC one-ton truck that Delbert said he had run last fall. Talk about luck!

The house was liveable. Five people had been living there, with the well situation allowing alternate bathing months. An oil heater was comfortable within a 10 feet area, with no lingering in the bathroom, which had no heat.

Mom immediately started her overhaul and remodel plans. Frank Lloyd Wright could have used that woman. I was just over 16 and, I might add, pretty naïve and inexperienced. I had run the old 10-20 McCormick-Deering tractor on our little 16 acre hillside farm to haul manure and mow some hay but Dad sold it before I tipped it over like Babe had to save my life. Boy, we could have used it on that old prairie flat land. So my story begins.

3

Brother Bub came home on leave from the Navy on a weekend and of course the 1928 GMC gave him no problems—it was running with no worries in short order. No one seemed to have any concern that I was just 16 years old and so was the truck. It was, simply said, "Chip, let's go get our stuff on there and move!" And because Bub had said I could, and Dad didn't know any better, I blithely drove it between places loaded with boxes, furniture, implements. With the good Lord looking out for me with every load, we did it. We were now, officially, nervous in Gervais.

The picture of those first days ain't pretty. First of all, we had never seen a milking machine, let alone know how to use one, and there were 14 cows to be milked night and morning. We learned fast. Every day punctuated with manure going on a pile the size of a mountain. Calves in a pen with crap accumulating all winter, skinny pigs (that I thought never got fat), four horses that needed care, and all this done in my spare time, after school. It gave real meaning to home work.

Do you know what had got us into this? R.W. Hogg, our very successful good farmer neighbor had told Dad one Sunday, "Just give me a dozen cows to milk, and it'll pay for any farm I'm on." When I learned that, I wanted to kill the old bastard.

4

We had hardly gotten our feet wet—as the old saying accurately goes—when dear old Mom started the turkey talk. Why this woman had turkeys in her head only God knew. It wasn't enough that I burnt down our brooder house where we had lived before, or that the turkeys got spooked one morning and flew across the highway into the river. Now she was figuring Big Time, with 1,200 turkeys. "Why, we can just put a floor in that old garage and brood 400 just like nothing, and then we'll put a brooder out in that old chicken house for the other 800."

I was raised never to question Mother. So project turkey started and using one old shed, I made the floor and tar paper covered the cracks in the wall. I cleaned out manure from the old chicken house and then we white-washed inside with water and lime mixture. Jack Gibson, our old neighbor, had a sister, Muriel, who gave us three big brooders. Bub wired the building and we ordered the turkeys. Of course there was one small item, #1 poults were 75 cents a piece, but we could get #2s for 25¢, so we got #2s. When they came, Mom and I dipped each little beak in water to give them a drink before putting them under the hover.

They started growing and eating. At first, I could haul the cow feed and turkey feed on our 36 Ford pickup from town. But it was soon evident that old "Jimmy" had to be put in service. Because it had dual wheels we assumed no limit to load. So I was hauling three tons at a time and can't believe to this day the only incident that occurred was running over a dog who was foolish enough to think I could stop.

5

All this time I was trying to move the Mt. Hood sized manure pile, cut hay, plow ground, milk cows, and do it with old fashioned horse power. The first time I hooked up a team to the mower after they'd been cooped up in the barn all winter, we did the first round in Kentucky Derby time, with me sitting on the seat holding the reins with very little control. It was then that I said, "To hell with this! We need a tractor!" This was in 1945, the war was still on, and tractors weren't being made, and used ones were very scarce. The only thing we could get was a "D" John Deere 1927 vintage on steel wheels, built when John was a boy. It was started by grasping a 800# flywheel and turning it over until one of the two cylinders decided to fire. It took a while, but it was Deere or horses. So I, with the help of the neighbor, got it running, almost every time I wanted it to.

The first job was getting the manure from a pile to the field. In the past, manure hauling was one horse with a sled and loading and unloading with an instrument named a manure fork, which should never have been invented. Well, with one cow producing manure, it wasn't a major task to distribute it to the land. However, with 14 cows, 10 calves, and 4 horses shitting all day and all night, the faster I hauled, the more behind I got. I never had a Christmas that ever compared to the day in May when Dad said, "I was able to buy the new Sears Manure Spreader. If you can haul it, you can get it." That was one trip old Jimmy made to town, maybe even making the speed limit. One side note: the spreader came with a long tongue for a horse team to pull. Needless to say, that appendage was shortened to tractor size immediately.

We hired a neighbor, Frank Bowder, to help load it by hand forks, but what an indefinable joy to see that spreader flipping crap. Sometimes it is the insignificant that is burned in your memory. I'll always remember the turds flying 20 feet in the air.

6

In early summer we bought a plow and of course, neither Dad nor I, had ever used a tractor plow before, but we had been told that a "D" would pull a 3-bottom plow. So that's what we bought. Two things were wrong: first, the plow wasn't worth a damn when it was new and hadn't gotten better with age. Second, when the French Prairie dries up, you have about a 12-hour window between too wet and brick hard. I missed that time span by about 2 weeks. When I finally got the plow in the ground, I was turning over dirt chunks the size of dog houses. But there was a hypnotic-like trance about plowing, and once I got going, I turned that whole farm upside down. I had no clue what I was going to plant, or how, but by God, it had gotten plowed.

One bright idea worth the merit of my always thinking Mother was a field of sunflowers for shade for the turkeys. So we planted sunflowers on the piece of ground I had fertilized, and we had it made in the shade. There were many hot sunny days that summer that the sunflowers proved to be good for the birds.

Another idea was to plant a field of corn. So that old truck "Jimmy" and I went and borrowed Hogg's corn planter with this big roll of wire for "check rowing." Dad had always heard that you should always check row your corn. That means you had rows running both lengthwise and crosswise. That may be the way in Nebraska, but after ten rows I said, "to hell with that! If I can get the seed in the ground I'm doing good." Besides, the corn field never got cultivated once, let alone in both directions.

7

The miracle of all this is that the tractor never broke down, the GMC always started and ran. The cows lived and gave milk. The turkeys grew fast. The sunflowers grew. The corn looked good. My old neighbor's "hired help" helped me with the haying. Like Smith-Barney, we did it the old fashioned way, which was tiring and stupid. We piled it in shocks and loaded it on an iron wheeled wagon to haul it to the barn. There was this ingenious device called a *hay fork*: two prongs, three feet long, jammed down into hay on a wagon and lifted to the loft by ropes and pulleys. Brilliant except the slick dry grass hay never stuck together and it took longer to unload it than to grow it.

But tenacity and stupidity won the battle. The loft got filled. In the process, we were able to cut the tip off Dad's finger and 20 acres of grass hay (I don't think he remembered the hay, but he sure didn't forget that finger). We cut hay with a five foot horse mower behind a tractor and raked it with a dump rake.

8

I was a junior in high school when this all began. Dad worked at Price's, a department store in Salem, and Jean worked for the State, also in Salem. Two neighbor girls also rode into town with them to work. Gasoline rationing was in effect, but with the farm exemption, gas wasn't a problem. I rode to town with them in the mornings, and when school was out, caught the Greyhound bus home to Keene Road in Gervais, so that I could get the evening chores done and be ready to milk when Dad came home.

Needless to say, my school social life lost some momentum, except when I took the pickup to bring home feed for the livestock. This routine continued through my senior year, and I became the last DeLapp kid to graduate from Salem High School. I wasn't a valedictorian, as I used study hall and the advanced algebra class to catch up on my sleep. Miss Boentje woke me up one time and said, "I'll have to speak to your dad about your sleeping in class." and I replied "I wish you would, he sure doesn't listen to me." When she saw her threat had backfired all she could do was laugh. I never got less than a "C" in her class afterwards.

It has occurred to me several times that I could have been given a little spending money, but I felt lucky enough to buy lunch.

9

With brothers Babe and Bub both overseas, you cannot have any idea how glad I was to have the war end that Spring in Germany and then that August in Japan. I could see help a-coming. However, during the war we did keep the neighbors laughing (and I guess they never stopped until we sold the farm). Bub got home in time to save the GMC from total disintegration. Babe got home in the middle of winter to find one John Deere "D" buried to the intake in my cornfield where I was trying to fence it (I was going to *hog it off*). We sold 1,000 turkeys at the top of the market, which only got Mom to figuring how to raise 5,000. The French Prairie story has many more chapters, but none as confused as that first year on the Prairie. We finished the remodel of the old house (damned near burnt it down with the old oil heater), drilled a new well, bought more cows, raised more turkeys, bought a new tractor, built new buildings, and got a "Grade A" dairy operating. And, I wasn't 16 anymore.

FRENCH PRAIRIE SAGA CONTINUED

As far as I can remember, the Shellitos just faded into the mist and never surfaced again upon us showing up and taking possession. I honestly believe they were afraid that, had they shown up after we were there for the first two weeks, one of us would have killed them. No way could a 16-year-old ignoramus and a shoe clerk ever get on top of that muddy mess, and their observations had merit. First of all, in the milking end of this neat, red, Gambrol-roofed, cement-floored, concrete, side-walled, cozy cow-odor barn, were 14 stanchions—7 on a side.

Now, I didn't know that each cow knew her place each night, and thank God they did or I never would have gotten to know each one. The barn was outfitted with a Sears milking machine—two buckets, vacuum pump, lines, etc. The drill, night and morning, was to wash the udders, extract the milk, strain the crap out into a ten-gallon shipping container, and then supposedly cool the milk down before shipping.

It wasn't until later (when we had water) that we used a portable, coiled water cooler that we stuck down into each can. The milk we sold was *factory milk*—which meant drink it at your own risk—it was for making butter. I never did know why shit in butter was alright, but nobody cared. We shipped two cans a day at first and when we started surprising the cows with grain and pasture we got up to four cans—Wow! The natural progression of a milk cow's life is to have a calf, be re-bred after three months, give milk for ten months, be dry for two months, and start the process all over.

With 14 cows and the breeding dates written on a post by name—they don't say "I'm Daisy"—one can only imagine the complete chaos that ensued. For instance, a cow who is supposed to be bred and isn't, and one who is not supposed to be bred and is. As the old saying goes, timing is everything, and you know it's off when you find a calf out in the barn from a cow you milked the night before. Ben Hall was a farmer and had good jersey cows and despite our inept management, they did produce. Our biggest unanswerable problem was flat land with no drainage, so that for every drop of rain that falls an inch of mud grows, and I believe that was a wet Spring. A cow in mud up to her knees is also in mud up to her teets and they have be cleaned. Oh well! Strain it twice!

BEN HALL'S BARN
I digress

I imagine when a music composer has a melody come to him, he has the compelling urge to compose music. It is the same when a vision of a life happening occurs and I feel like describing it. So it is with Ben Hall's barn. When we bought the Ben Hall farm in Gervais the outstanding feature was the barn. He was a farmer, loved animals, milked 15 cows night and morning, and farmed with horses instead of a tractor because, he said, "They would always start." He was a simple man, but like most of us, he had a history of pride and creativity. When there are 15 cows to milk, one must get up at 5 o'clock to ship the milk at eight. That time of the morning in winter can be miserable and it had been the dream of Ben to build "The Barn." Often some men vision a new fancy auto or a big house or Hart Shaffner and Marx suit, but Ben put together this magnificent barn far above any other. He consulted draftsmen, Oregon Ag College and other builders and dreamed of this for years, until one morning he told his hired man, "Today we start the barn."

It wasn't a quick overnight project but the methodical Ben had the plans and the more it progressed, the clearer the vision. At the same time his 110 acres needed farming, but every day some work was done on the barn. Concrete forms for the floor, timbers laid on beams, upper floor joists, rafters, cedar split-shake roof. Instead of the old rotting floorboards he had concrete and manure gutters with drains to an outside tank and a pump that took the effluent out to a field. The old siding with the cold blowing air was replaced with concrete walls four feet high with 14 stanchions in the milking room that was warm and cozy. He liked lots of light so the full length of the milk room was windows. There were four stalls for the horses with hay mangers and three calf pens. Two grain bins to hold enough grain for the year, the hayloft large enough to hold all the loose hay for a year with a hay pulley system to eliminate the pitchfork. Sliding doors on each end to close it up tight. And to put the topping on the cake a new Sears milking machine. When Ben went to work at 5 o'clock in the morning and opened the door to the milking parlor there was the nice pungent aroma of warm animals being very comfortable. This was all Ben needed or hoped for. It was no longer a chore, it was pure pleasure. It had taken him a year, he had done it. He had erected the monument to the legacy of Ben Hall and for years to come he had the most beautiful red barn in the area. It exemplified who Ben Hall really was.

TURKEYS

When we lived on Dallas Highway, mom had a thing about chickens and turkeys. Now if there is anything dumber than a turkey it has to be someone who raises them. Our venture on the Dallas highway ended abruptly when we burned down the brooder house with a borrowed oil brooder. But we saved the turkeys—30 all told—and learned that brooders should be electric. So what do we do on the prairie for a big, one-shot money crop? Turkeys! Very simple: 1,000 turkeys, making $5 a piece, and *voila!*—five thousand dollars! But don't forget that you have to work hard and worry lots, scrimp and save, and then we'll make five thousand dollars (what a stick and carrot game that was).

All we had was the idea; no brooders, no brooder house, no money, and no help—but we had Chip, thank God! I don't have total recall or I would be in intermittent depression. The family said, "We can seal up that old chicken house and put two brooders out there, and take those old boards and make a floor in this old garage for another, and we'll get 1,200 poults, and we'll make $5,000 dollars." So we got three big, electric brooders, got the old buildings wind-proof, and in comes the big day.

You can't imagine the difference between 50 (our previous capacity) and 1,200 of these dumb little brown things. We maybe weren't too bright but we did have experience raising turkeys. We knew we had to dip each beak in water and put them under the hover and then put colored marbles in the feeders to direct them to the food. What we didn't know was just how long it takes two people to dunk 1,200 beaks.

They grew great. We learned that our open air brooder system with ventilation was ideal and that too close confinement isn't good. Another thing we learned was that because number ones were 75 cents a piece and seconds were 25 cents, we bought seconds. Some developed a leg weakness and couldn't walk, but overall our losses were minor and we did have some eight week old fried turkey (just don't ask why those legs look funny).

From there on out it just became a problem of logistics—out to range and water and feed—and that was every day. One thing about turkeys: fencing them in wasn't a problem. I think if a wire could be placed head high, they would be too dumb to go under or too dumb to go over. When they did wander out, we had little "Spot," our Australian shepherd, who loved to herd turkeys, so she would be right there to put them back in the pen. One of my most vivid recollections is on the rainy, sloppy day we sold the turkeys. Spot slogged through the mud up to her belly, herding them up to the catching pen until every last one was loaded and she was exhausted.

The finality of the venture was the price of the turkeys. It was the highest they had ever been, we had nearly 1,000 to sell and we made over $5 apiece, and in the end we made our "five thousand dollars," which of course, was all the fuel needed to do it again.

I have emphasized the five thousand dollar goal. This is important only being relative to past farming income; the big one-time yearly loganberry crop we harvested, hoping for a five-ton for which we got $50 a ton, or a gross of $250. We paid ten cents a crate for picking—and that was only for outside help—and all the other work of plowing, training vines, hoeing weeds, putting back vines and cutting old canes was all covered by family unpaid labor. Easy to understand a steady milk check and a turkey pay day as an incentive to do the deeds—we had been brainwashed at an early age.

SATURDAY AFTERNOONS

Lying in bed early in the morning causes the strangest thoughts that at the time are very revealing and make perfect lucid sense. Later, in the reality of broad daylight, by poor recall and loss of the moment's revelation, they may lose the importance of vivid flashback color that was so clear and moving at the time of conception. Out of the blue recesses of the foggy, dim recall process of this strange mess of human computer chips now comes a totally new and completely emotionally accepted revelation of the lifelong feeling of contentment and pleasantness associated with Saturday Afternoons.

In the memory pattern of emotion and events, Saturday afternoons always come to me as a pleasant time. Today I have a hard time considering Saturday afternoons as anything but a time to enjoy doing something of insignificance, of pleasure, of some time-wasting, and without guilt, time to squander.

As a kid, I suppose without thinking of it, the end of the week had some let-up in terms of school stress. We got chores done in the morning, and Saturday afternoon was a time-recess before the start of the next week, which began with a somewhat *Daddy-at-home* structured Sunday and starting school on Monday.

In the summer we always went swimming on Saturday afternoons. When we went on our annual vacation we left on Sunday, and so Saturday afternoon was exciting. It seems we never picked berries late on Saturday afternoons. If we went to town, it was Saturday afternoon. We always made cider, dressed a couple of chickens, or did other things preparatory to enjoying ourselves, on Saturday afternoon.

It was always the Saturday before Christmas—at least a week before Christmas—that we went Christmas tree hunting. Our farm extended into the acres and acres on defiled pasture with growing trees. We never thought of or knew how you could buy one, it was always just, "Time to go find the Christmas tree." It had to be six to eight feet tall, fully branched and star receptive top. This subdued excitement of the *Perfect Tree* will always be remembered, and Mom would always rebuild that excitement with, "Oh kids, that's a beautiful tree!" So Bub would build a wooden stand and we would tinsel and decorate with ornaments.

I also remember going to the UCLA–Oregon State football game to see Kenny Washington play on a bright, autumn Saturday afternoon. Even though I liked to listen to football on the radio, I didn't often do it on Saturday afternoons. Rainy Saturdays were when the ferocious Monopoly games took place in the basement by the furnace. Those were pleasant memories because I won my share.

When I was in the army most training stopped at noon on Saturday, and the rest of the day was free. Maybe it was the start of a short weekend, or, more likely, just a goof-off, do-nothing, no-planned few hours of regeneration. I have an uneasy feeling that perhaps I missed some enjoyable part of raising my children by not creating the do-nothing Saturday Afternoon syndrome. Should I have made a memory pattern for them? Did I do enough in that respect? I hope I did. If I didn't, what do I do now?

Those reflections could be elaborated on, and even though the most traumatic happening of my life occurred on a Saturday afternoon—another story for another time—I can only think good of the day. I did survive.

THE ARMY – CORPORAL PUNISHMENT
A Cynic's View of War

W hen you consider that the simple solution to fighting a war is to draft a 22-year-old cow-milking, naïve farm boy and to try to make a soldier out of him to fight a hungry little Asian, who has been trained for ten years in how to kill someone, it's probably the stupidest idea ever invented by mankind, but—by God—we've tried it several times. I have always maintained we never ever fought a smart war and the only reason we whipped the British in 1776 was that their method of fighting a war was marching 10-abreast across an open field wearing red coats with a boy playing a piccolo. Our strategy has always been, draft a lot of men, and let the enemy kill us until they run out of ammunition. Then we capture them and feed them until they can start another war.

When we fought another country, we outnumbered them, out-produced them and simply overwhelmed them, but in our Civil War, we fought each other until dumbness prevailed on both sides. We slaughtered 600,000 men for five years and since the North was the biggest buyer of South's cotton and since the South was the biggest buyer of North's ammunition, when the South ran out of cotton and the North ran out of bullets, we ended it. But one event we didn't stop: breeding. We always kept a fresh supply of men growing up to fight another dumb war, which brings us to Korea.

So, in 1950, five years after ending the greatest war of all time, I'll be damned, the politicians start another war. So here I am, 22 years old in October, single, farming for my life, feeling lucky to have been too young for the World War II and here comes a friendly letter in the mail saying, "You registered for the draft four years ago and we want to conscript you for a little *police action* in a country called Korea (wherever the hell that is).

It seems in our efforts of ending World War II, our brilliant negotiators let Stalin talk us into dividing the Korean peninsula into North (Communist) and South (Democratic), setting up the perfect situation for a civil war, which the Communists had planned. So the mountain people, ruled by Russia, not knowing Communism from cornflakes, think it a neat idea taking control of the rich, productive rice fields of the south. Well, we had started re-building the South and told them, "By God, we'll defend you from these no-good, dastardly Communists."

So they sent this little letter saying, "David DeLapp, we need you in this army to go 8,000 miles across the Pacific Ocean, and take you from milking your cows to ensure these little Asian people can keep growing rice." It was our misfortune to have re-elected, in 1948, as our Commander in Chief, the same brilliant strategist who had been duped into getting us in this position. So, he sends an *advisory*: 200 soldiers to stop those 50,000 Red soldiers. They were immediately killed or captured, so old Harry, ex-artillery, WWI veteran, says, "Hey, you guys want a war? By God, we'll give you one." So he drafts David and 40,000 other men into an activated National Guard division and with all that surplus WW2 equipment. Who knows, *maybe I can get re-elected again to stop another war.*

David is not brave, he is not courageous, he is not willing, and he didn't volunteer, but if all the other 22-year olds had to go, why should he be deferred? So, he went. He said it took four others, two pulling and two pushing, to get him in the army. They put a rifle instead of a pitchfork into his hands and soon changed overalls to overseas.

SERVICE IN JAPAN

"What the hell, if the army wants to give us an all-expense-paid trip to the Orient, what better time for a single man than when I'm 22, with probably not another chance in my lifetime."

This was the joke, the façade hiding our real trepidation and confusion about the reality of being on a troopship heading for Japan in 1951. Six months before, I was secluded in my own little world of day to day coping on the farm, trying to make a future. With the start of the Korean war, that little world got bigger in a hurry. That quick transition from overalls to overseas is what makes Japan the most unique place I've been. Getting there was no Holland–American cruise; what with 2,800 troops crammed on a converted Liberty ship, none of us had any concept of our role in the damned little war we were getting into.

In early March we arrived in the *Land of the Rising Sun*, but instead it was a *Land of Falling Snow*, so our first realization was that the weather there is much like it is in Oregon. Our first comment and the most readily apparent, was on the small stature of the average Japanese and how intimidating 100,000 troops—mostly of over six feet tall—must have been when dropped in their midst, especially just five years after losing the war to us.

How does a person begin to appreciate the beauty of a country or its people while being homesick, confused, ignorant of their customs, and unable to talk their language? How difficult to appreciate the fact that these little people were just farmers and fishermen who from their viewpoint were accepting our intrusion into their lives with as much confusion and disruption as we felt. Regardless of the propaganda during the war, the Japanese are inherently friendly and compassionate people. At no time, even on a pass to the big cities, did we ever feel hostility.

Spring in Japan is like spring in Oregon—trees leaf out, gardens are planted and growing—and that springtime feeling of release from Winter affects all. Many festivals celebrating blooms and blossoms give the people days of partying, singing, parades, and exhibiting the marks of their centuries-old customs of dragons and tigers and weird costumes.

We looked, we laughed, we exchanged the greetings we had learned in a hurry, and gradually settled down to learning about where we were. This wasn't a one way street: they tried as hard to learn our language as we did to learn theirs, maybe more motivated because we had money to spend; silk jackets and bamboo fishing rods were bargains no GI could pass up. On reflection, we probably gave them their first ideas in how to salvage the defeat from the war and sell those Americans *always a bargain.*

THE CRUISE, 1951

I experienced it all—the Northern rural country and the big city commercial atmosphere of Tokyo. Along with the sights to remember are the smells. Big city or small, the stench of open sewers, open fish markets, honeywagons, and their strange cooking odors, took some getting used to for an Oregon country boy. I was there ten months, and although leaving it meant going to Korea and right into the war, that wasn't why I was reluctant to leave. The country was pretty, the women were beautiful, the people were gracious and friendly, and there was more I wanted to experience, but that's life—always a little more left to do. My journey into that big world outside had opened my eyes and what I saw was nothing I couldn't cope with.

In my previous essay I have described our one year occupation of Japan. In January 1952, we landed in Pusan, Korea, in 22 degrees below zero weather, with the main problem not being shooting anybody, but freezing to death. Canvas tents are not the best insulation against weather cold enough to solidify diesel heating oil.

I was lucky enough to be drafted into a radio platoon of a communication company for the regimental headquarters of the 160th Infantry Regiment, operating a radio net for all the line companies in the 160th. We were to consolidate all communications with a radio network between our regiment and the othe two regiments, as well as the three battalion headquarters and line companies 24 hours a day. We also supported tank and artillery companies with spotting aircraft. The fighting 40th infantry division was an activated Los Angeles national guard unit. It should be noted that this unit was mainly comprised of out-of-work Mexicans who drew pay for attending a meeting once a week, conducted by WWII leftovers getting paid looking for retirement. The fighting 40th had more fights in bars than wars. The year we trained prior to Korea weeded out most of the imcompetent by attrition only to be in-filled by ROTC officers who in college never dreamed of serving in an active duty.

The next seven months in Korea, the 40th Division maintained its position, had a battle line perimeter extended and had the hell scared out of us by having the enemy sneak in through the command areas, killing people, and raising hell. One of the constant reminders that there was a war going on was the continued night and day artillery bombardment that was to our rear, firing 155 millimeter shells over our head with some exploding in air. The command, "Wear your steel helmets," didn't have to be repeated.

CORPORAL WITH CONVERTIBLE

The positive side of this experience was that for two years, the same 75 men shared their lives in close confinement, mostly in two squad tents. Sol Arditti, son of a Jewish clothing store owner in New York, with the pretty little wife whom he had just married, worried about her faithfulness, and we didn't help him a whole lot by our obscene suggestions of what she was probably doing.

He wasn't the only one. While the majority of us were unmarried, the married ones had anxious moments and worries between mail calls. For two years there were very few secrets and we were a close group of men, an experience I never had before or again, and that matured and broadened my horizon. To this day I can feel and understand that comraderie which millions have had by service in the military. They inducted me on my birthday and two years later discharged me on my birthday. So David DeLapp came home after carrying a carbine for two years, never shooting anybody or being shot at, but definitely a grown man whom the politicians would probably boast had "bravely and with honor protected the United States of America from those damned Communists." In the process they killed 50,000 of our finest young men in the Korean War. As in any war that was ever fought, we have to believe it was for right, and today us old veterans celebrate. We should—we are still alive.

GOD SAVES CHIP

I don't intend to explain God, but don't you think He may intervene sometimes just because one of us is so different that He has to see what else we will do in our lifetime and we just need more time to do it? This phenomenon is described as Guardian Angel or Gift of God, and I don't know beyond my own experience, but there are four accidental escapes that have allowed me to become 87 years old. Up until the time I was 24 years old I hadn't experienced any life-threatening events and God knows there were several opportunities in that time, starting with us all swimming in the river throughout the entire summer with nobody drowning. I returned after two years in Korea without being hurt, so coming home to live in Colton was the first place of four significant happenings. I don't know how we can say God saves us from a from life threatening encounter and not at the same time ask why he put us in that position. I labeled this essay "God Saves Chip" but have to wonder for what did God save Chip, and the only thing that can occur to me is that He wanted me to write this book. So that puts this right along with the Bible.

The first event is what I have titled 'Roller Coaster,' which was an event that I extricated myself from. The second event, tipping over a tractor, was also one, and though I broke my leg, I didn't get killed. The third event I didn't survive on my own volition. Of the four accidents, number three is one I cannot take credit for saving myself, as I did in the final event I have entitled "The Life Changer." In saving myself there is pure wonder and thankfulness and acknowledging that God gave me the idea of how to get out of it. These accounts I have written about and I have to leave it to the reader to explain.

ROLLER COASTER

The first event is not so eventful but quite imaginable. It was 1953 and I was back from Korea, 25 years old, farming and custom hay baling all over the hill country of Colton with a John Deere Model "A" tricycle type tractor and a very heavy "80" New Holland Baler. My brother had warned me from his experience previously, to be very careful coming down grades with all that weight pushing a very poorly braked tractor. I had finished a job about 2 p.m. and was moving to the next, which was about two miles down a long hill on Meadow Brook Road, a 2-lane paved road.

I started down, thinking the compression of the tractor engine would keep me going slow. But, it started faster and the engine began revving too fast. I started braking and both wheel drums started smoking with me gaining more speed. I knew I could do nothing to stop it. I had two options: bail out and let go, or take it out of gear and let it roll. I chose the second one. I knew it was a long hill and at the bottom was a 4-way intersection with the main highway. The old adage of "it's all downhill from here" isn't always the happiest to contemplate, and I had no idea that I would go as fast as I did. I took it out of gear and off I went, a two-ton tractor meant to go 12 mph, with a 3-ton baler with no brakes, coasting down a curving road gaining uncontrollable momentum every foot. If ever there was a time for divine guidance now was it. This was a high profile tractor with 38-inch diameter tires, so here I am sitting five feet off the ground, wind whistling past me, guiding this out of control vehicle going 50 mph and faster. If I jumped it would certainly have been the end of me. So, I held on for what seemed an eternity (scared that it would be) and God only knows how fast I was really going at the bottom of the hill. But with my luck, He stuck by me, with no cars on the highway, and I coasted through, out onto the level, and came to a stop. I was at least 20 years older and shaking with fright.

GETTING TRACTION FOR 20 YEARS

The second experience was with the same tractor in 1954 with a loader bucket mounted on front, which, when raised high, creates a weight and leverage that makes tipping over much easier. I took off on a logging trail with the loader up and came to a water filled hole, and not knowing it was three feet deep, the front of the tractor went through but when the rear right hind wheel went in, started to roll. I bailed out as quick and with as energetic jump as I could manage to make sure it didn't roll over me, but in doing so, I kicked the one-inch steering bar that runs along the top of the tractor. I knew when I landed that I had broken my leg. My brother, being nearby, ran to me, relieved that the tractor hadn't rolled on top of me, and then ran to get the car and took me to the doctor. The major importance of this event is that I wound up marrying the nurse who took care of me while I was in traction. It took 20 years to get over that accident.

COLTON

The Colton phase came after being exposed to the adult real life or other inhabitants of this world in the Army—a million dollar experience. I wouldn't give ten dollars to do it again. Mom and Dad fed me, kept me warm, provided shelter but were very little help in coping with the other people in this life, other than by example. I was totally unprepared for the culture shock of being suddenly taken from the solitary life as a farmer milking cows, with minimal social outlets to being lost in an army division of 40,000 other solitary individuals for two years, using only my God-given ability to make it.

I found quickly those other people weren't relation, they didn't know me, and really had no reason to know me. I discovered I could make close friends, could attract strangers, could handle inept authority, and could be adult. So I came out of the army a different man than the French Prairie narrowly-focused kid. As a birthday present I was drafted 10/15/50 and discharged 10/15/52 at 24 years old.

The Colton farm was a foothills stump ranch with a big beautiful white barn and a rundown log house and a 32-foot dug well. My sister's husband, Sam, was in the logging equipment business in Eugene and he estimated there was 1/2 million foot of salvageable timber, so all at once my brother Babe and I were loggers, chainsaw and all. From October til Spring, we had the Winter to plan a strategy. Dad hired Hugh Evans with a small portable mill to start cutting cants sold to Kapler Mill. Babe and I salvaged pulp logs for the Oregon City Paper Mill. In the spring of '53, I used my savings from my Korean duty to buy a hay bailer for $3,500, New Holland wire tied, best on the market. And so began the hay day of the Colton era.

We baled hundreds of tons of hay and grass seed straw. Started buying heifers and without thought or brains were back in the dairy business, refrigerated bulk milk tank and all. With logging, dairying, clearing grounds, building a hog barn—raising grand champion Hampshire pigs—we were two busy men. Hugh was an Okie with a half-wit brother in law (which exaggerated the ratio somewhat). His favorite quote was, "Leon, you can do the damndest things." He made lumber out of anything over six inches in diameter, but mostly out of good logs and trees that previous loggers had left.

Brother Babe and I then salvaged the leftovers for pulp woods with a farm tractor and a two-ton 1948 Ford farm truck, getting $30 a ton for wood in eight-foot lengths for making paper in Oregon City. We hauled five tons with God as our co-pilot for 25 miles without an accident. That was at $150 a trip, three trips a week. With a good new barn, featuring a 20-stanchion milking parlor, we started our second dairy.

In order to get hay for our livestock we cut, raked and baled on shares, usually for half. One clover field was 60 tons 35 miles away. We baled hay all over the country and filled our barn cheaply and did custom baling for money. In that grass-growing country we were busy.

Getting killed logging and hauling hay wasn't sure enough, so we decided to clear some 11 acres of cut-over bottom land, for which we had irrigation right from a creek running through it. The project: Use a couple sticks of dynamite buried under a stump, which, when blown apart, could be pushed to the side of the clearing. Why or how we got through all that with all of our body parts intact couldn't have been because of our smarts, but after we hired a D-7 dozer with clearing teeth to clear the field, we picked up roots and limbs, plowed it with a disc plow, planted rye grass and clover, and put a small gas irrigation pump on the pond we had made on the all-year creek, and raised the most productive pasture ever imaginable.

An interesting side comment to this process: Years before, the Swede farmers on the adjoining land, with lots of lumber, few brains, and unimaginable hard work had built a flume out of sawn 1×12's, made water-tight for probably two miles, crossing our farm from the artesian outpouring from the side of the hill , irrigating about 200 acres, plus for house and livestock domestic use. It had fallen into disrepair but still remained as testimony to their ingenuity.

There are some accomplishments you either brag about or try to hide, and most of them came from ideas formulated by lack of funds. Such was the octagon silo. In Gervais we had two round wood stave silos which provided storage for corn silage and pea vines for wonderful dairy production. At Colton, a lumber producing area, there were several stud mills which had eight foot 2×4's not good enough to sell which they discarded by the truckload at firewood price. Our ingenious idea (mine) was: "Let's built an octagon silo, with laminated boards, airtight, 30 feet high, with windows on one side to throw down the silage," which we did.

No one can imagine how many boards it took to build a 30 foot structure an inch and a half at a time. But a pyramid builder could have given us a clue. We got it built, we filled it with green chop from our newly cleared field, and we started milking cows, with the monthly All-Jersey milk check. Maybe not too smart, but effective.

My marriage and Babe's marriage created three families living off one farm, so the Colton experience ended after six years. After selling the Grade-A dairy with registered Jerseys and each heading for our next adventure, I was strictly on my own. Philosophy: There are two sights on a gun, hindsight and front sight. In hitting the target you must use both. Colton presented many options that we used. I made many decisions every day, most of them good, some of them bad—but none with regrets. We matured, we innovated, we gambled, but most of all, we learned we could handle any situation that may arise and the rest of our life was better for the Colton era.

So what could happen to the busy scenario? In the Spring of '54 I tipped a tractor and rolled over in the woods winding up in traction in the hospital with a broken leg and marrying the nurse and having three kids. Thus begins the Scotts Mills story.

CHICKEN VENTURE AT SCOTT'S MILLS

I f we get smarter by our mistakes, I should be a genius. I've made enough. I'm always impressed by the acclamation, "From the time he was five years old he wanted to fly a spaceship, and now he's doing it." For me, all my achievements have been accidents and my failures well thought out. Most notable perhaps, was the great chicken gambol. I have to believe no child pondering his universe and future ever said to himself, "I want to grow up to be a chicken raiser, and clean eggs and haul manure for the rest of my life." But when opportunity knocks on that door of stupidity, it's hard to turn away. It all started before I was born.

My mother had a fowl phobia. I was raised feeding chickens, watering chickens, shoveling manure, and raising turkeys (that's a whole different earlier episode), so when I shrewdly took advantage of this clearly stupid real estate salesman, I ended up owning a 19-acre, two thousand hen egg-laying setup. It never ever occurred to ask why the seller had abandoned it and moved to town and went to work for the state, defaulting on the mortgage. Could it have been no heat in the house (or insulation), a dug well with one bath a week limitations, and an accumulation of three years of manure in the chicken houses? I sure slickered that old fart. The setup was three brooder houses, a converted, pretty little round-roofed barn, and a newer large free-range building for 1,200 layers.

I knew almost everything there was to know about chickens (my mother raised 100 at a time): You put feed and water in one end and eggs come out the other. So when this feed salesman tells me about his General Mills program to buy chicks, furnish the feed delivered, buy the eggs, and get paid back (with accumulated interest), when the egg money came rolling in every week I said, "Sign me up with those chicks (I found out that figures do not lie but liars do figure)!"

I cleaned up the buildings, got the four 500 chick brooders working and—oh happy day—the day of delivery came. Through some lack of perspective vision, I didn't realize just how many 2,000 of those little bastards are. They come 100 to a big cardboard box, and twenty boxes is ten feet high. The correct way is to dip each beak in heated water before placing them under the heated hover. I said, "You'll have to find those waterers on your own, I'm putting you all to bed."

Four hovers, 500 to a hover and they did great. They needed a gradual reduction of heat for six weeks, then they feathered out and were ready for the great outdoors. My 19 acres had an oak wooded area ideal for summer shade, but also ideal for chickens to roost, so after the first few weeks, my oak trees looked at night like big cotton bushes filled with 2,000 white Leghorn chicks, not quite the recommended method by the feed company field man, but they were beautiful healthy birds.

When at five months it came time to house those hens, I invited the two field men to my catch-and-release party. "When you sold me this program you said anytime I needed help just call," so now, catching chickens and carrying them to the laying house was just the help I needed. Like any healthy mature females, they started laying eggs, and I do mean by the bucketful. As a frame of reference and to help you visualize the enormity of my underestimation of my undertaking, a five gallon paint bucket holds about 300 eggs and a daily lay of 80% is 1,600 eggs. So, every frigging day, seven days a week, every egg has to be cleaned, and they had to be dry-cleaned. This ingenious cleaning machine is a narrow conveyer belt running between two rows of whirling sand paper rings that produce a beautiful polished egg. So here I am, setting these eggs on one end of the conveyer, about 40 at a time, then rushing to the receiving end, putting them in 30 dozen crates. If you ever saw Lucille Ball's chocolate factory routine, I repeated it every night till midnight, and never laughed once.

At the end of the tunnel, theoretically, I sell the eggs, the feed company takes their cut, I stay home, mind my flock, clean my eggs, and make a living. Well, the theorists and the feed salesman never raised chickens in their life. The reality is, I had to go to Portland and get a job in the daytime, and clean eggs, thaw frozen pipes, milk a cow, feed the hens and the family. Our diet was lots of protein like fried eggs, egg salad, soufflé, and angel food cake (12 eggs). The days were long and tedious, the weekends short, but I was young. To add to the problem was this killer. The feed company's agreement was to have a market for my product, picked up at the farm, but their outlet quit after the first six weeks, so they contracted another who paid me directly, with bad checks. Well, needless to say, the feed company also didn't get paid. That's when I learned bootlegging didn't have to be just whiskey.

I found a couple of big apartment complexes that liked farm fresh eggs, so before I began my sales job, I made a few bucks delivering eggs. Of course, all this good luck couldn't last. On my way to work one foggy morning at 7A.M. on September 16, 1958 I was broadsided at an intersection by another vehicle whose driver admitted to going 70 mph, in a dense fog. The impact knocked my Plymouth 76 feet sideways, shearing off a 10-inch light pole, and landing in a small country cemetery. A passing neighbor stopped to help and tracked me down by the indents in the grass, where I had bounced 112 feet from my car. I was unconscious with my scalp laid back, bleeding. The old farmer who found me later told me that he had turned to the rescue team and said, "Well, you might as well just leave him where he's at." The write up in the paper the next day described me as critically hurt with head and chest injuries, and broken bones. In reality, all I suffered was some loss of blood from the scalp injury and a displaced thumb. I had come through without so much as a broken bone. My scalp was stitched, and a small cast applied to my thumb and after two days in the hospital, I was discharged home. Although the report to my family was that I had been killed, in fact, as Mark Twain said: "Reports of my death were grossly exaggerated."

Although I was only laid up for a few days, my old dad and mother, and wife, had to do the chicken routine, after which she said she came a lot closer to killing me than that Buick. After I continued this routine of character building for a year, I arrived at the conclusion that I should have raised fryers, which gives a break every eight weeks. So half-a-million clean eggs later, I sold the hens, paid off General Mills, started selling real estate and thought I had retired. Fifty years

VOLUME FORTY-FOUR.

Barlow Crash Hurts Two; One Critically

Thrown 112 feet from his demolished automobile after it sheared off a utility pole, David DeLapp, 30, was critically injured Wednesday about 7 a.m., following a collision between his car and one driven by James George Ballweber, 25, at the Aurora-Lone Elder intersection with the Barlow-Monitor highway.

DeLapp has severe chest injuries, several fractured ribs and head injuries, and was taken to Willamette Falls Community hospital by Canby ambulance. Ballweber returned home after treatment for chin cuts and knee bruises in a Canby physician's office.

The intersection was shrouded in fog, according to Ballweber, an airlines employee who was en route to Portland airport from his Monitor home. He said the fog caused him to drive to work, rather than fly, as usual, from Jack Lenhardt's Ninety-One field.

DeLapp was traveling the Lone Elder road toward Aurora and the Baldock freeway, on his way to work in southwest Portland as a bookkeeping equipment salesman. Father of two children, he lives in the Marquam-Scotts Mills vicinity.

While Firemen Norman Christiansen and Jack Trusheim were moving the injured DeLapp from the Barlow Lutheran cemetery into which he was hurled from his car, two other cars were involved in a lesser crash at the scene.

Wallace Peterson, 43, of Needy was not hurt when his car struck a parked vehicle on the Barlow-Monitor road. The parked car was registered to Peter Borgen, who also lives in the Needy area.

State police were summoned.

later, I look back on those times with nothing but thanks it didn't happen again, and that somewhere in his afterlife there is a feed salesman spending his eternity cleaning eggs.

2

GAINING GROUND
AND ROUNDING THE FIRST TURN

THE CHANGE OF DIRECTIONS

Few people have the good fortune and foresight to have a predestined future. When I was young—milking cows, baling hay, raising chickens—if anyone would have suggested I would be a fairly successful real estate broker, altering and affecting many other people's lives, I would have said, you better count your marbles again because I think you have lost a few. It took me a few years to realize everyone is interested in real estate. Rich or poor, owner or renter, everyone has to live someplace. So without much contemplation, I got into a business where everyone was a customer. And all I had to do was satisfy their wants and needs. Their need is a roof over their heads—a cave. Their want is to have a little nicer cave than the neighbor.

So there's where I came in. I know of a bigger cave with a private room to sleep with your partner, then another for the kid's cave. So, soon, what happens but Crazy Chris, your country caveman, is finding and building caves. Fifty thousand years later, he's building sub-divisions and hotels and needs an out of work cow worker who knows how to deal with people. That's me.

Then came the bright idea of a government man who saw the need to invent honesty. So he starts a bureau to oversee my honesty and charge me a fee for a license to do business. Of course, he has to hire an out of work used-car salesman to oversee me. Despite the regulations, fees, inspections and bureaus there is no saturation point in the real estate business. Competition yes, but everyone is your potential client: business buyers, sellers, developers, new owners, retiring owners, (don't make the newsboy mad, he's your client in 10 years).

And the important fact: He will find you if you are honest and truthful, and a good Baptist will add, "And go to church." Church goers believe in God and the 11th Commandment: "Own your own home."

A large segment of the real estate business is created by people changing positions, selling to buy something else so I found an ideal situation, which is to find two parties who have each other's property. I put together an exchange. This became so prevalent, especially in the tight money market, that we formed the Real Estate Exchange Club with members and clubs all over the state.

State of Oregon
Real Estate Agency

THIS IS TO CERTIFY THAT THE PERSON NAMED HEREON IS LICENSED/REGISTERED AS PROVIDED BY LAW AS A

LICENSEE: **REAL ESTATE BROKER**

DELAPP, DAVID L   **No. 780303062**

DELAPP REAL ESTATE
45849 RIVERLOOP RD
PO BOX 483
LYONS, OR 97358

ISSUE DATE
07/01/2002

BY: OREGON REAL ESTATE COMMISSIONER

EXPIRATION DATE
10/31/2003

BROKER THAN BEFORE

ADVICE

I think possibly the worst person to give advice to is a young person, and probably the worst time to receive it is when we are young. I had a very progressive grade school teacher who sat down with me after school, before I graduated as the only one in eighth grade, for a long talk. Probably the only time in my whole life that anyone has ever given me real advice. She thought I had a talent for writing and encouraged me to follow through. Ruth was homely but was a teacher before her time. When I got to high school I got "A"s in English and a couple of times had the teacher and the rest of the class regaled with laughter with my humorous reports.

As we get older we don't get advice—we get suggestions that the giver intends to be advice. The best example of the most significant suggestion of my life that I took was from my oldest brother. I was having a hard time finding my niche after leaving the dairy. "Chip, why don't you sell real estate? My church friends Leo Reiman and Ed Lucas have an office and I think they will hire you." They did. That was March 1960, fifty-five years ago, and, as the old saying goes, "I haven't worked since."

As a broker, I found that advertising was writing, and I was able to use the skills Ruth had encouraged in me years ago. My newspaper ads soon became noticed by others in the business, which helped in the beginning to enlist cooperating brokers in the Multiple Listings Bureau. To this day I still get comments on some of my presentations. I have saved a few.

One piece of advice I didn't take was after working for my first broker Leo. He called me into his office and, with his good old Baptist fatherly manner said, "Dave, I don't think you are cut out for this line of work." I said, "Thank you. Jacobson and Keene have offered me a job as their farm salesman and I won't have their brother-in-law getting first shots at the prospects." I changed offices and, two years later, became my own broker for the next 45 years.

P.S.: Four years after his astute advice, Leo declared bankruptcy. Sometimes we take the right advice.

POCKET CARD—SALESMAN   EXPIRES JUNE 30, 1962

STATE OF OREGON
REAL ESTATE DEPARTMENT
This Is to Certify

THAT DAVID L. DELAPP

HAS BEEN GRANTED
A REAL ESTATE SALESMAN'S LICENSE TO ACT ONLY WHILE EMPLOYED
BY LLOYD G. KEENE
A LICENSED REAL ESTATE BROKER.   SALEM

CITY   OREGON.

6220 LICENSE NO.   ISSUED BY ORDER OF
12-22-61 DATE ISSUED   REAL ESTATE COMMISSIONER
TO EXPIRE JUNE 30, 1962   OF THE STATE OF OREGON

VOID UNLESS HOLDER IS EMPLOYED BY BROKER ABOVE DESIGNATED

POCKET CARD—ASSOCIATE BROKER EXPIRES JUNE 30, 1963

STATE OF OREGON
REAL ESTATE DEPARTMENT
This Is to Certify

THAT
DAVID LEE DeLAPP   HAS BEEN GRANTED
AN ASSOCIATE BRUKER'S LICENSE TO ACT AS AN ASSOCIATE BROKER
ONLY WHEN EMPLOYED BY LLOYD G. KEENE
A LICENSED REAL ESTATE BROKER.
SALEM   OREGON.

CITY

A-356 LICENSE NO.   ISSUED BY ORDER OF
16 OCT, 62 DATE ISSUED   REAL ESTATE COMMISSIONER
                          OF THE STATE OF OREGON

VOID UNLESS HOLDER IS EMPLOYED BY BROKER ABOVE DESIGNATED

USE YOUR CAR, boat, lot, equity, mother-in-law, anything, as down payment for this better built 3 bdrm. home, north. Beautiful lot, curbed street, carport, dining rm., breakfast nook, 2 baths, wall to wall carpet. REDUCED $2,000 to $14,750. Use any type of financing. DELAPP REAL ESTATE 364-0077.

JUST MARRIED?

Cheer up, your luck should change by buying this home. What could be nicer; cold cuts in the pretty built-in kitchen, a roaring fire of old wedding bills in the fireplace, the in-laws comfortably settled in 3 large bedrooms & extra large family rm. for who knows what . . . and all paid for just like a marriage "A little down & the balance as you enjoy it." $14,500. DELAPP REAL ESTATE 364-0077.

NICE HOME FOR NICE PEOPLE

I think, when you see this, that you will agree this is one of the prettiest places in the suburbs of Salem. With all the desired elements of 3 bedrooms, built-in appliances, dining room, large living room, raised hearth fireplace, 1½ baths, double garage, it has in addition those quality items that turns a house into a home Let me show you. If you are tight with a buck, the price will be a pleasant surprise, only $15,950, which is $1,000 below FHA Appraisal. Owner can't take another wet winter. Call DELAPP REAL ESTATE 364-0077

SELL, rent, option, trade. Real pretty 3 Bdrm home. Northeast adjacent to city limits. Fireplace, pretty kitchen, covered patio, double garage; a good place for kids. $12,699. $2,000 equity. Good terms, consider trailer house or lots. DeLapp Real Estate 364-0077

66

EDGAR HOBART

The Scotts Mills 19-acre chicken farm was a good buy and we were never uncomfortable. And it was a learning experience. It was a country community, with no Meier & Frank on the corner. I had the whole area to myself and one of my first clients was Edgar Hobart. He lived in a dilapidated old house with just one dog, in one room with a wood stove. Hobart gave the definition of "filthy rich" real meaning. He held mortgages and contracts that went all the way from Silverton to Molalla, and hadn't had a bath since he was baptized. The dog left home three times looking for cleaner places. Why I appealed to him I never knew but we became friends and I sold property to him and for him with never a quarrel about commissions.

It was just my first year working at a nice downtown office in Salem when the broker said something about this dirty bum walking by looking in the window. I said, "Ed, don't call the cops, that's my best client. It just hasn't rained yet." Edgar realized he wasn't presentable in the office so I went outside and did business with him on the sidewalk. After I moved to Salem I lost contact with him, but learned when he got sick— probably ate some bad dog food—that the hospital attendants swore Doc Heckerd had said, "Put him on a gurney and run him through the car wash."

He was related to the executive Hobart at Ladd and Bush Bank, and there's a road named after him in Silverton. He was a nice, honest little man, maybe a little dirty but sharp as a tack. He hadn't accumulated his wealth by being dumb. I've often wondered about who bought his property after he died and how much money did he find buried in tin cans in his yard.

SHORTY

S horty was a gift, kinda like an old tire someone discards in your front yard in the middle of the night. On this Sunday morning about a month before Christmas, there he was, an all-black, mostly cocker spaniel, sitting on our lawn with those big, sad, soulful eyes; long ears, short legs and friendly wagging tail that said, "I'm a good dog. You will like me, and I'm an orphan." Well, we had a small dog. We lived on a small lot and one was enough, but like sunshine on a winter day, "Shorty" was too good to be ignored. He worked the old charm and soon had three kids petting and feeding him, without the slightest idea they were being conned. Shorty became part of the family despite my admonition that one dog was enough.

A serious problem arose with our planning a trip over the Christmas holidays in which my brother had reluctantly agreed to take care of our little dog (but not every stray in the neighbourhood). Using that as a legitimate reason, I said, "I'll take Shorty to the county animal shelter so that someone can take him home as a Christmas present."

Comes the morning, I'm to do the old hand-off trick. I call Shorty and open the pickup door. In he bounded and sat on the seat, wiggling all over, and looked at me saying, "This is fun, where are we going today?" God how I wished he wasn't so eager to please. When we got to the pound, in he went. There were pens of dogs of every description, especially cute puppies, pretty long haired dogs, beautiful collies, big, small, all clean and ready to go home with the next owner. But here, hugging close to my leg, was short legged, long-eared, sad-eyed Shorty saying, "What are we doing here?" When the very pleasant woman said, "You may leave him and if someone doesn't choose him in a week, we have to euthanize him to make room for more coming in." I looked down at Shorty and realized he wouldn't have a chance. When he looked up at me with that little trusting face, I said, "I've changed my mind," and back to the old pickup we went. "You will just have to spend Christmas on the farm with my good old brother, he'll like you just fine."

I'm in Business!

Written in 1965. An open letter to renters I have come into contact with and selected apartment complexes.

Dear Mr. and Mrs. Renter:

I want to sell you a home. No beating around the bush, no double talk, I would simply like to be remembered by you as the man who convinced you, to buy a home.

There are valid reasons why some people should rent for the time being, such a temporary job location, transferring, single and not settled, etc. To these people I say, wait a while.

To everyone else, the ownership of your home gives you a stature, a permanence, and independence and respectability as nothing else can do. Ownership of a real property is the basis of all you will possess in your lifetime. There are many more intangible reasons why a deed is more to your benefit than a rental agreement and there are many plain old dollars and cents reasons. Here is one:

If you now pay $95.00 per month rent, there is a non-deductible expense forever gone. But look what happens to that $95.00 as a home payment. A $95.00 payment will pay the principle, interest, taxes and insurance on a $12,000 home. Sure, the first year approximately $80.00 of the monthly payment will go for taxes, insurance and interest, BUT these are all deductible from your earnings as a living expense, and the balance builds your equity. You are actually affecting a savings of about 35%, based on a low tax base, and you have enjoyed the comfort of a private home, garage and yard.

If you want to discuss your future in owning a home, please call or stop in my office. In helping you select the right place, price, terms and type of financing, I need to know you. I will recommend no home until we have met face to face. It's as important that you know me as I know you. No other salesman will call on you, as I have none. You will at all times be dealing with me, a Broker, Realtor, Trader and Member of Multiple Listing.

I have the property for you. Buy now. As the price of real estate continues to go up, your equity becomes worth more and your debt becomes less.

Let us at least get together and talk this over.

Dave DeLapp
DeLapp Real Estate

State of Oregon

Notarial Commission

To all to Whom These Presents Shall Come-Greeting:

Know Ye,

That I, **Tom McCall** Governor of the State of Oregon, reposing special trust and confidence in the integrity and ability of ___DAVID L. DeLAPP___ do appoint ___him___ a **NOTARY PUBLIC,** in and for the State of Oregon and do authorize and empower ___him___ to execute and fulfill all the duties of that office according to law, and to have and to hold the said office, with all the powers, privileges and emoluments thereunto legally appertaining, for the term of four years.

In Testimony Whereof, I have caused the seal of the State to be affixed at the City of Salem, Oregon this 16th day of ___July___ A.D. 19 68

Governor

Secretary of State

BY THE GOVERNOR:

COMMISSION EFFECTIVE___July 16, 1968___
EXPIRES MIDNIGHT___July 15, 1972___
SED Form 787 (Rev. Sep. 1967)

TO WITNESS YOU ARE NOT DEAD

72

RENEWING MY BEGINNING

On Dissolution of Partnership.

In 1965 I and two other brokers formed a partnership DeLapp RE Brokers Association. "Cap" Capwell had been a salesman with me for 2 years, Ted Rohde had been a farm salesman for Rawlins Realty, and I had an office. We operated out of my location and it worked, but when a dispute happened, Ted withdrew and Cap went on his own, while I was back a to one-man office—I did my own thing.

December 6, 1966

Ted:

Maybe writing will exclude all the emotional complications inherent in different viewpoints that is getting beyond the bounds of justified disagreement. We have been friends of a degree that transcends just a business relationship; this I feel is worth preserving. I believe this is more valuable than mere money, and shouldn't be destroyed by the interference of our needs in worldly possessions. However each man has been given the individual right to select the importance of friends and the value thereof as compared to money, and no other person can make this decision for him. Cap has told me that as of last night it is your decision to withdraw from our business association. If this is a final decision of yours, I accept it with regret. I'm sure you have given this careful consideration, and in your own mind are sure this is a positive action for your personal benefit, that cannot be gained any other way.

This is not the first instance in which an association that started with good intentions has ended with poor results, nor will it be the last. The important part, to my way of thinking, is that the dissolution is done as intelligent and amicable as possible with the preservation of respect for each person that has existed through previous years. If we cannot do this then we have disclaimed all rights to call ourselves adult.

We both recognize the unequivocable fact that the present status is attributable to the settlement of Brant – Smith commission. How else can we decide except with the question: Did Dave DeLapp contribute 25% toward the consummation of the total transaction, at your request? This decides the degree of division. The amount left after notes, Brokers Fund, etc. may have everything to do with your participation in the association, but nothing whatsoever with the responsibility on present closed deals. I don't think there is any dissension in regard to your participation in the broker's fund. This a bookkeeping matter and I favor an equitable distribution of the same.

When I made the transaction on the Sunnyview Dairy, it was with your agreement at that time to receive 10% as Finder's Fee, when resold. Because of the small likelihood that this will happen very soon, this will be paid immediately, on settle ment of all points in question.

We think alike on a lot of things. I think we can help each other in the future. I need all the friends I can get.

Dave

July 20, 1965
Mr. Campbell Steketee
4810 Coloma Dr. SE
Salem, OR

Dear Sir:

This is a notice that I hate to write and have put off writing for 2 months, but in the interest of good business must write now.

As you know, taxes, property values, and expenses have come up in the last year on all real property and so as of a necessity, I have to increase the rental payment of the house you now occupy, to $110 per month.

Because of the fact that I wasn't the owner when you rented the property, I have hesitated to increase the rent, but it has cost me money out of pocket.

In relation to other rental rates on houses, I feel that this is in line, and still good value for the money.

This will become effective August 1, 1965. If you feel this to be too much for you to pay for rent, please let me know when I may expect it to be vacant.

If you are interested in a purchase, of this property, I will allow you $25 per month credit of your occupancy toward the down payment.

Yours Truly,
Dave DeLapp

INTRODUCTION TO INFLUENCE

Salem, Oregon
April 10, 1963

Allen Jones
Chairman of Arbitration Committee
Salem Board of Realtors

Dear Sir:

I would like to know my position in the following matter, in relation to Part ll, Article 20, Code of Ethics NARES;

On April 9, 1963, I, Dave DeLapp, Broker of DeLapp Real Estate, and member of Salem Board of Realtors, presented to Richard Grabenhorst, broker of Grabenhorst Bros., at his place of business, 180 Liberty St. SE, Salem, an Earnest Money Receipt together with a check in the amount of $5,000.00 for the farm belonging to Albert Ramseyer and others, located on 95th Ave. NE, Salem. This offer was drawn up by me at the request of the purchaser for the expressed purpose of a starting ground for negotiations, and was the first and only offer signed by him, up to this date, for purchase.

On presentation to Mr. Grabenhorst, I was informed that the offer would not be accepted by him, as one of his salesmen had also been working with this same prospect, and that he would have to talk with the same salesman. When I contacted Mr. Grabenhorst at his home that same evening, he emphatically declared he would not present my offer to the seller and that "If the buyer wants that property, he better make it through our office," further adding, "this is our listing and we will do with it as we please."

Mr. Grabenhorst said he would contact me the next morning after conferring with his salesman in person, which he never did. On the afternoon of April 10, I personally called at the Grabenhorst office and left a note for Mr. Grabenhorst to call me, which he never did.

On April 11, I informed the purchaser that his offer would not be presented and cancelled it at that time.

I shall be glad to present these and other subordinate facts to the Board, and abide by their ruling.

Respectfully,
Dave DeLapp, DeLapp Real Estate

As an added postscript to this offer I must say that actually Rich Grabenhorst did me a favor by being a big shot and by not accepting my offer. I was able to find a farm that suited my client much better in an area that he liked, so it worked out better for me and it worked out better for him. Grabenhorst went broke in the business by his arrogance.

Choosing the Wrong Help

Circuit Court of the State of Oregon
Third Judicial District – Marion County
February 13, 1969

Jerry G. Kleen
Attorney at Law
210 Pacific Building
Salem, Oregon 97301

Steve Anderson, Attorney at Law
468 State Street
Salem, Oregon 97301

Re: DeLapp vs. Cooper, No. 64662

Gentleman:

The above entitled matter was tried to the Court without a
jury on the issues raised by the plaintiff's Amended Complaint seeking a real estate commission and the answer of
defendant, and at the conclusion of the evidence, the Court
took the matter under advisement.

The evidence offered at the trial discloses that there
is no question but what the exchange properties between
defendant Cooper and Oather Tripp was effected after
the expiration of the listing agreement, plaintiff's exhibit
one, but within the 90 day period immediately following
the expiration. The sole question to be determined then, is
whether or not Oather Tripp was placed in touch with the
defendant during the term of the listing agreement. On this
question, the evidence is in direct conflict. The plaintiff has
the burden of proof on this disputed issue of fact and the

Court feels the plaintiff has failed to sustain his burden of proof and that the plaintiff, accordingly, is concerned about sales being consummated after the expiration of the listing between the owner and prospective purchaser with whom the broker has placed the owner in contact, it seems to the Court the broker could better protect himself by some written memorandums evidencing the contracts and acknowledgment by the owner during the terms of the contract, rather than relying solely upon oral assertions after the fact based on memory.

Very truly yours,
Douglas L. Hay
Circuit Judge

Note: Jerry Kleen and I graduated from Salem High School in 1946. I found that didn't make him a better lawyer.

February 13, 1969

To the Circuit Court Judge, Douglas Hay on the Trial for Suit of Commission:

Dear Judge Hay:

I determined immediately after trial I would write this letter, but would wait until you rendered your decision before mailing so it could in no way affect your decision regarding RE: DeLapp versus Cooper, in which I was the plaintiff. I know that as poorly as the evidence was presented, I couldn't expect anyone to reach a good decision. In my opinion, of the three legal men present, you were the only one fully aware of all of the facets of the case and asked the most pertinent questions of the witness. I don't think my attorney ever got the facts straights. I was convinced you were trying to get to the crux of the problem to enable you to make a fair and just decision. I sincerely thank you for your impartial attitude and what I feel was a conscientious attempt to do right. I only wish my representing attorney had had half your understanding (thank God he wasn't representing me in something serious). The only redeeming thought is, I believe the other attorney was probably as inept as mine, so we should have flipped a coin. I know I was right, but I cannot rightly criticize the court's decision. You just weren't given a hell of a lot to base a decision on.

Yours Truly,
Dave DeLapp

In a subsequent case of lease default by a lessee, I think this letter helped. Judge Hay ruled their testimony was fraudulent and ruled in my favor.

3

THE 70S: AN ERA OF CHANGE AND HITTING MY STRIDE

MY BEST DEAL
1968

I had lived on a farm all my life up until I moved back into Salem, into a very comfortable three-bedroom house—the best home we'd lived in up until then, but on a 100-foot lot. It was very confining; the neighbors were very close and it seemed my kids were next door more than home, and I didn't think they were raising their kids the way mine should have been raised. When I was a kid, I always had the responsibility of taking care of animals and a garden, so with the four years living on Bell Avenue I never lost the sight of getting back to the farm. I then had my own real estate office at Center and Lancaster. Being a member of the Multiple Listing Bureau, I noticed the 7.5 acres of an expired listing (3 months not sold) on Lancaster Avenue.

Immediately I went to look at it and found the old retired couple ready to move. Talk about a dream come true. Why it never sold, I'll never know to this day. An English style 2-story home, 3 bedrooms with a den and full basement, fireplace, hard wood floors, formal dining room, breakfast nook, beautiful manicured backyard with a brick fireplace with a rotisserie, double garage, 20×40 shop, cute barn with loft, irrigation and well pump, and 1.5 acres bearing filberts and apple trees. To a 70 year old man it had become too much, for a 40 year old ex-farmer it had everything, including being just 24 blocks to my office and the very reasonable price of just $28,000. On that first look-through I said, "Mr. Larkins, I'll buy it." He said, "Your wife hasn't even seen it," to which I replied, "If she doesn't like this she'll have to stay where she is alone."

Larkins took a rental house equity and $21,000 cash which George Wilton at the US Bank easily agreed to, "Dave, if you don't buy that, I will." I moved out of Bell Avenue to 3080 Lancaster, our home for the next several years. Lancaster Drive was then a 2-lane country road but all of East Salem had a sewer system completed and hooked up. So, now started the kids' learning experience of animals—a pony—peddling produce, picking nuts, raising a garden, irrigating pasture, and all those living experiences with responsibilities, the only way I knew how to teach. It wasn't but a couple of short years until Lancaster was widened to five lanes, development quickly began and our neat little farm became surrounded by subdivisions and commercial enterprise. It became glaringly evident by this one late-night incident.

WAKE UP CALL

B elieve me, nothing can get your attention quicker at 2 A.M. than a whirling red-blue light in your driveway and someone pounding on your door. Jumping out of bed, not entirely decent—and not entirely coherent—I opened the door to this uniformed sheriff. My first thought to his questions, "Do you have some cattle?" was to deny any ownership as I suspected this wasn't just an early morning livestock survey. I had trouble. "They are out in the street and are running through this shopping strip near Silverton Road." Hollering at the kids to get up and help me, I grabbed pants and shirt, put on shoes and headed out.

Sure enough, there they were. My first action was to head them off toward a big open field across the street from home with tall grass, ditches, brush, and pitch dark. When watching four heifers led by a young black yearling kicking up their heels and running loose in a 40 acre field one loses all compassion for Martin Luther King's "Free, free at last!" Then came the bull horn which could be heard into the next county, "Mr. DeLapp, they're heading South, and we'll stop traffic 'til we get them back." Well hell yes, they're heading South, and so will I if I don't have a heart attack or step in a hole or break a leg when I get them headed back. I have experienced many satisfactions large and small, all of which led to life's enjoyment. But none could surpass that sheriff blasting—heard all over the east side of Salem—"Mr. Delapp they're back across the street and heading toward the barn."

Maybe the return of the wild wanderers to home was a stretch of divine guidance and so I thanked God. Someone had left a gate open upon doing chores the night before and I'm sure the kids were relieved from expectations of dire retribution when they heard their dad re-counting the early morning activity with howls of laughter about the heifers strolling through the shopping center looking in the windows of the beauty parlor and crapping in the drive-up lane of *Tasty Freeze*. As the old cliche states, I literally had a wakeup call. We were in town. No more playing farmer here. The time had come to change the focus of our 7-acre farm. The livestock were sold and soon after the land was sold to developers for apartments and an athletic center, leaving us with just memories to laugh about on every gathering.

It turned out my impetuous spur of the moment judgment was the best decision I ever made, and that included selling to an investment group to "locate" their courthouse athletic center. I had taken advantage of the old saying, "Location, Location, Location," for ten times the amount I purchased it for. After the family was grown, I ultimately—five years later—bought a 13-acre farm close in, for half my selling price, and could pee on my land without my neighbors seeing me.

BULLDOG FATHER

When we had the farm on Lancaster I tried to keep in mind the old farm background that I had to teach my boys responsibility for taking care of animals, and so I bought a black Angus cow and her calf from my previous neighbor Harry York at Colton. I brought that cow and calf down to Lancaster where I had a lot of pasture. The calf was sucking the cow, growing healthy, and I had a nice little barn for them. After I'd had this pair for a couple of months, this bull calf was a typical Black Angus, weighing about 400 pounds and square as a refrigerator. One evening when they were in the barn, I said I'd to like catch that calf. I don't now remember why, but I had a reason. My sons Mark and Jay were standing outside of the doorway to the barn, and it had rained so there was manure around the front of the barn door.

Inside the barn the Black Angus cow and calf were eating, so I stood blocking the doorway, kind of showing off to the kids what dad could do. When that black calf saw the door was blocked, he came at me like a 400 pound fullback through a linebacker, knocking me flat on my back into the mud and crap and went right over the top of me on out to the pasture. Mark stood there witnessing the whole action and for all his might he tried to keep from laughing, but he doubled up with laughter. It was the funniest thing he'd ever seen. So there we were, me covered with crap, Mark and Jay in convulsions, and all I could do was swallow my pride and join them.

Trading Property and Wives

How do you tell a story without having a beginning? (And there's nothing more boring and dis-interesting than the beginning of an uneventful ending). So, the story herewith has a beginning that I'll start sometime after birth, like 32 years. Now, the 32 years had their moments of interest but that's another boring story. My first excursion into the real estate business was taking a tractor, on a small farm I had sold, as the commission and everything has escalated from there.

Exchanging was my forte. I purchased my first good house on Bell Avenue with a 100% loan and the seller paying all costs and I getting commission. I traded my Scott's Mill farm sales contract for a ten-unit apartment complex in Salem, and took third leg properties and made trades as my commission. That had only one drawback. Orvill Roth still wants cash for groceries so commissions still paid the bills. During this time, I made a trade of a small house with $21,000 cash for 3080 Lancaster. 7.5 acres, big three-bedroom with full basement, double garage, 20×40 shop and a cute round-roofed barn. By far the best deal I ever made in the real estate business. The family house, room for animals, ideal location to peddle produce, close to my office, and a pride of ownership place to live—I was shifting into high gear. All the horse trading was paying off.

It became apparent to me that during hard times of getting cash money, exchanging was a alternate way to sell property, and getting my feet wet with my Scotts Mills trade for the apartment house was the beginning of me doing many trades. Thereafter acquiring the Lancaster property we moved to, I continued doing the same thing and acquired a 2 ½ acre property on Auburn Road, which I ultimately added another 2 ½ acres to and did my first subdivision. Simultaneous to this I took in trade for a commission a house on Illinois Street, which was occupied for a couple years later with the forming of a partnership. I then took a 7 ½ acre property in Keizer from my attorneys, which they agreed to let me develop without buying. I ultimately used it to build Kennedy mobile home park.

Simultaneous to this my partner and I acquired 13 acres on Verda Lane in Keizer in which I subdivided. It was a commercial property; I divided it into parcels and sold the lots. So this began the many operations of many trades, which all worked out fine. There were duplex lots, and in Northeast Salem 13 houses that traded for our 28-unit apartment house. The apartment complex of my partner traded for the 100-space mobile home park—just one of numerous exchanges that I put together that benefited everybody.

They tell me it was during a depression time, and I have always said that monetary cycles never bothered me. I had a hard time when things were good. As an ending to my exploits I will go back to my purchase of the Lancaster property which I have said was the best real estate deal I ever made. I ultimately sold it without trade to a development group for an athletic center for ten times the amount that I paid.

AT FIRST SIGHT

In 1966 I traded an old house in Portland I had acquired for an old house in Salem. On August 13, 1966 who walks into my office but this friendly, laughing, warm divorcee named Snowman (honestly). She was an RN at Salem Hospital, with two small kids, moving from Manzanita, 35 years old, and built like the proverbial farm expression. With the first month's rent she was my tenant, with the unbelievable fact of a house at 2345 Summer Street rented to a snowman. One rule that I had made up and strictly adhered to was not to mess around with any renters or any other woman. So, although I probably did more personal maintenance on the Summer Street house, I didn't use or abuse the tenant. We had some nice appropriate conversations but no hanky-panky.

Patricia always seemed to like coming into the office to pay her rent and talk, but she had her social life, so no sparks were flying. One incident I remember vividly was that I had a chance to trade my equity in Summer Street for a 25-foot Chris-craft yacht. When I showed him the house, Patricia was in a halter and short shorts, and he nor I could keep our eyes on the house. She had legs, boobs, and body. In December 1968 she got a job at OHSU in Portland and moved. I sold Summer Street, thought about her a lot, but thought the third act of the play had ended. One day in late Summer of '69, a note was on my desk. Patricia had stopped in to see me, leaving her phone number. So, I had meant more to her than just the landlord. I called her and the romance began, marrying on August 13, 1975, nine years to the date after I had met her.

FELIX

My first wife and I believed in the institution of marriage, but after 19 years, as the old saying goes, neither was ready for an institution. We liked marriage, but not to each other, so we separated. I had built 16 rental houses, so I moved into one.

I had never lived alone, kept house or cooked for myself in all my 46 years, and it must have been evident because one morning on my patio sat this pathetic-looking, cross-eyed, long-haired Himalayan cat looking me in the eye, saying, "Feed me and you and I will be friends for life." I did and we were. I had a hot dog in the fridge and a piece of carpet inside the garage door for his bed, so I didn't adopt Felix, he adopted me. I had company soon sneaking into the living room until put out for the night. Felix wasn't selfish: he shared with me very often his mice, birds and moles all laid nicely on the patio by the door. When I started feeding him regularly he became a handsome cat despite being cross-eyed. He never got in trouble and I never had one complaint from the old age retirement residents across the street. Felix was a one-man cat.

For my divorce settlements the ex got 16 houses and I kept the cat. Luckily, my second wife likes cats so she and I and Felix lived in harmony in a house in my old neighborhood for two years.

We then moved back to the farm that I had on Lancaster. I was concerned that Lancaster had become a 4-lane boulevard with heavy traffic. It got my little dog but not old Felix. We lived there a couple of years with him, feeling he must provide for us to the extent of coming to the back door with a live, fully grown China Pheasant which we ate.

After Felix had been there about six months, we kept coming home and finding the front door, which we never locked, open. We really didn't know who was opening it until 6 o'clock one evening, when we heard the latch click on the door. It swung open and in walks Felix. He could just stretch and reach the handle and pull down the latch. So, what the hell, we locked the door and gave Felix a key. After that Felix stopped showing up. After three months I had given up and feared something had happened. During that time I made up my mind never to have another animal subject to such a busy street, when one evening six months later, scratching on the door, was Felix, well-fed, well-cared for. Someone had taken him in their house and never let him come home. Here he was, fat and sassy. I swear he was strutting.

I sold that property and moved out into the country where, in his old age, he didn't have to cross the street and could hunt and sleep any time, but of course he had one more trick. My sliding patio doors also had a sliding screen on it. It wasn't two months until Felix would have his claws in it and pull it aside four inches and come in to the house on his own. He became an old pest and lived out his life there. I've never had one with such a personality since.

MINNESOTA MIRACLE

I had been in the real estate business as a broker six years, sublimely experiencing borderline starvation, with my own one-man office in a shopping center east of Salem. As with any business with an unlocked door, you never know who's going to come next, so one Monday morning the maintenance man for the shopping center, seeing my name on the window, came in and asked, "Do you have relatives in Minnesota?" to which I replied with a small smile, "If they are rich I think so, but otherwise I don't know of any." "Well, I was born and raised in northern Minnesota and a Delapp was known as the only person to have trapped a white fox." "I'm sure if any of my relatives ever trapped a white fox it would be in the family Bible," I said, "so I'll have to decline that notoriety." And so our conversation went on to him saying that he still owned 127 acres in Minnesota that he hadn't seen in the last 35 years since he had last logged it.

He was talking my business so I was mildly interested and asked, "What is that land worth?"

"Well a broker there has option to buy it for $1,200," he replied.

My fantastic computer brains immediately calculates, "That's less than $10 an acre!"

"Yes that's right," he said.

"Well is it on the bottom of the lake?" I asked.

"No, it is covered with timber that has grown for 35 years since I last logged it, including a few old sugar maple trees and I've got some aerial photos of it," he answered.

"Well, if what you say is true and that woman with the option doesn't want it, I'll buy it."

The next morning he was waiting for me with the photos and the news that the woman did not want to buy. The photos showed a two-story barn next door casting a shadow that showed the full acreage covered with trees taller than the barn, with the main highway dividing it into 120 acres on one side and 7 acres on the other, sitting adjacent to a resort a stones throw from Lake Itaska with seven resorts. What sane or insane broker could pass up such a deal?

I mortgaged my oldest child, wrote the happy man a check for $1,200, executed the Abstract of Title, and became a multi-state real estate investor, site unseen. That kind of a deal hadn't been made since we snookered the Indians out of Manhattan for $24. The only negative aspect was my wife, who wanted to know, "You bought what? Where? For how much?" Waking me up at one o'clock in the morning she asked, "Where in the hell is Northome, Minnesota?" Calmly I answered, "Near Itasca Lake in Itasca County, one of ten thousand in Minnesota with taxes only $64 a year."

This was in 1970, and in 1976 I had a new wife. We were married by a judge (I should've asked for a jury) and she wears a hearing aid, so when he said "for better or for worse" she thought he was giving me advice and said "forget her for a nurse."

With 1976 being the national Bicentennial I said, after owning this property for six years, it's time we saw the rest of the states. We reversed the Old Oregon Trail to Minnesota and with new wife and 16-year-old son we headed east with a car and travel trailer. After seeing the wonders of Glacier National Park, Yellowstone, the Black Hills, and Mount Rushmore, we arrived the second day of July in Northhome Minnesota, another wonder and not really an unpleasant site.

It was green, lots of lakes, warm and pleasant, and we could hardly wait to see the purchase. I had the name of the adjoining neighbor so when I knocked on his door he couldn't keep from laughing about that guy from Oregon buying the Nelson place, site unseen. He was Nelson's cousin. He was very cordial and willing to show us the property, even saying there was a black bear on the back 40. We soon found out about northern Minnesota. 40° below zero in the winter is not the bad part, but bugs in the summer is.

Those woods contain every insect God invented and everyone of them was active that day, July 3, 1976. Northhome has recorded 50° below zero winters, the cattle stay in the barn. In the summer the heel flies, bot flies, mosquitoes, and every other insect incubate and seek out anything with blood in it, and the cattle stay in the barn. Could this be the reason for $10 land? The only reason to live there was to be able to brag about being able to survive.

July 4th was celebrated by the local natives with a neighborhood potluck picnic, and they very cordially invited us to join them. Well, with most of the conversation being about the hail destroying the wheat up north and Zeke buying the new snowmobile, there wasn't much for us to add, except, "What in the world would people from Oregon come here for?" And there was no good answer for that one, so we ate their potato salad, fried chicken, Jell-O, and chocolate cake, thanked them very nicely and then left in a hurry for Duluth Minnesota, leaving them all laughing about those people from Oregon.

The conclusion to this insanity can have its positive side. I owned this piece of heaven or hell, whichever you want to choose, for 22 years. I never owned another piece of real estate that I got as much notoriety out of as Dave's Minnesota forest land. The standing joke of the realtors trading club for anything that appeared for exchange, however outlandish, was, "Will he take northern Minnesota? It comes with a black bear and sugar maples."

My last laugh came in 1992. The real estate woman who gave up the option for the $1,200 sold the 120 acres for me to a timber company for $35,000 and the seven acres on the highway to a resort on the lake for $8,500. And I had seen it only twice. No one got malaria and I had 1,000 laughs. I still have the second wife. On reflection of the people of Minnesota, there are probably no nicer people, kinder people, than the ones I met in Northhome. They were gracious and very friendly, but from the standpoint of reflection on the people who live in Minnesota, it is much easier for me to understand their electing a professional wrestler as a governor and the observation that Einstein didn't come from Minnesota. And there are a lot of people in Arizona with a Swedish accent.

INVOLVEMENT

This was written in 1970 when I was the PTA president of Hayesville grade school, of over 500 students.

Dr. Charles D. Schmidt
Superintendent of Schools
Maynard C. Shiffer
School Board Chairman
Administration Bldg.
1309 Ferry Street SE
Salem, OR

Dr. Schmidt:

We are writing this as representatives of Hayesville Parent's Club, and in doing so, solicit your acceptance of our proposal, herewith.

The Hayesville School has an area, of about 5 acres now unused, large enough to provide for every recreational activity needed by the whole community; unfortunately, the lack of needed facilities has been postponed for lack of funds budgeted for school ground improvement. We parents and other interested parties of this area think it a waste of assets and potential that the major portion of the grounds are not playable or used for any purpose. We therefore ask your permission to proceed with a planned phase development of this ground done by the concerned residents and parents.

We have asked and obtained from the Parks and Rec Department a rendering of a proposed overall project and suggestions from their professional staff on what might be done. Their engineering department has laid out a step-by-step procedure for the 1st phase which is development of a good playable ball field to be used in summer programs as well as during the school hours. Future phases will be development of an environmental project consisting of various state trees and shrubs and products; a regulation 90 ft. baseball diamond for Jr. League play; a jogging track for anyone's use; a broad jump pit; and even a horseshoe pit for the older adolescents of Hayesville Community. We would be very grateful to be able to show the members of the board the layout on the next meeting on February 26 and explain how we will proceed, along with our reasons why we think this ground should be developed as the center of the community.

It is our proposal to make this a community project, soliciting labor and services from every source including the students of Hayesville themselves who will be the direct benefactors. With the students becoming involved in the work and planning, we feel they will have more pride and protect it from abuse.

With your permission to proceed with the project, the executive committee of the parents club will present, as soon as possible, our concrete proposal to all the parents of the area, with their approval and commitment, we can have a community project, inexpensve from a budget standpoint, but an asset to the school and the neighborhood.

It is our hope and planning that before the school term ends, to also work out a system by which the school library can be used and manned part-time throughout the summer vacation.

We are soliciting no funds from a governmental source but with a demonstrated interest of the citizens, and a definite interest of the parks and recreation division, we hope the impetus started this year will lead to a cooperative venture for the future. The existing buildings lend themselves ideally to widespread community use, for many different programs.

The board gave overwhelming approval. We scheduled a work day in which all the parents turned out. I got a donation of a large dirt mover which "leveled the playing field." We installed underground sprinklers and turned an eyesore into a neighborhood effort of pride. Caroline Blake and I pulled it off successfully. UNBELIEVABLE !

This P. S. is written April 22, 2015, 45 years later. That neighborhood improvement worked; today there is a regulation baseball field and other areas, used extensively by the school and public.

THIEF: A COMMUNITY CONCERN

A kid stole my car out of my garage. Written when president of the local PTA.

Today there is a thief in our neighborhood who, last night in a matter of a couple of minutes, caused $1500 of damage to two autos. The auto damage is repairable, the damage to the thief is irreparable. Unless some straightening is done to his (or her) warped frame, I will not only have the cost of my auto to account for, but will bear the cost of penal custody for many years for the offense. If he is caught now, maybe something can be done, or if not, he will go on until his life cannot be salvaged. He will be totaled out. It's time we start looking at ourselves and our neighbors. Isn't it true that we no longer say we're unlucky if we have something stolen but rather we're lucky if we don't?

With all the money in the world, we cannot hire enough police to stop this disease. We must know where our boy is now. We must know why he comes in late at night with a hurt arm or bump on his head. We must care about that next door kid that carouses late at night and drinks too much. We must interact with our decent neighbors to apply neighborhood social pressure on undisciplined children and have guts enough to say to those parents who now are too damned lazy to raise their kids right, that we, as just plain people with property, are not going to idly stand by in a passive role while their progeny tear everything to hell. It is their responsibility, and we better start as a group pressuring these irresponsible people make the change or get out of our neighborhood. Shape up or ship out.

Happy Birthday to Vanessa 1973

Dear Daughter:

Happy Birthday!

What an experience you have been to me, watching and helping a beautiful fat little baby grow from a dependent being to an independent, self assured young woman. An experience not without frustrations, anxiety, and even doubts at times of my worthiness to be your father. But how proud I have been of your development in character, intelligence and sensitivity to other people. I think 17 is the beginning of a maturity of feeling and thinking in life that sets your course for the rest of your life. 16 is too young and 18, you have passed the point of beginning. At this time your character is reaching a status, a level that determines how happy a person you will be in your life, and that's all I can hope for and work for you to be happy in your life. I truly believe you have the capacity for unlimited happiness, but your course includes giving happiness and comfort to others. I would like to think, maybe this ability is in some way inherited. How nice it is to see the good parts of oneself birthing forth and radiating from its child. Of course, some other traits, not so desirable, will have to be considered as inherited but you're learning to handle roles within yourself much better than I.

Your mother and I wanted nothing more than a daughter who would mature and be happy within herself; that's the ultimate goal in living. We have that daughter. Writing gives one time to formulate and solidify ideas and feelings that are difficult to say outright, even though the feelings are always there. So my wish for you sweetheart, be happy with this birthday. It can be the rich beginning of many, many more.

Dad

LETTERS FROM MARK

Mark started Pacific Lutheran University in Tacoma. He thought he might play football.

February 4, 1977

Dear Dad,

Well, I made it. Here I am. After a complete day of classes I can say, I might possibly make it. Already thought, I've had some close calls – like driving up the other day, it was almost tempting to drive right by PLU . . . and keep on going. Canada if up ahead, a fanctuary for uf fchool dodgers. But I suppose you might not grant amnesty as easily as Carter did, so I avoided temptation and proceeded to the PIT.

As I mentioned I got my classes: Economics, 20th Century American History and an Argument and Debate class, and in the last ½ semester a Scuba Diving class (that should be alright). The first three I listed are going to be tough. But I'm still determined, I have already started studying – so there is hope.

I'm sending my registration to my car to you, because I thought you might want to change it to your name. Considering that we're going to try and sell it this summer, either put it in your name, change the address to my correct one (455 Cameo) or send it back to me – whatever.

Also I left my room key down there. It was on that old black key case, for the green pickup. Would you track it down and mail it to me? Thanks.

I just took a few minutes from writing this letter to play a little Foos Ball. IVX now has two tables in the dorm. I'm getting better. Even if I flunk out I will finish the semester with a pretty good Foos Ball shot (it's not that easy, believe me)!

Well, I guess that's about all I've got to say now. Say hello to Pat and if you ever feel generous, don't hesitate to send money.

Bye now,
Mark

QB stars in 1st start for Celtics

By BOB HUNTER
Capital Journal Sports Writer

Coach Larry Miller and his McNary staff may have to find a new term to describe Mark DeLapp, who until Friday night had filled the backup spot at quarterback.

Second string definitely doesn't fit DeLapp, as he showed in leading the Celtics to an impressive 35-7 victory over the Franklin Quakers. Replacing injured Tom Fox at the helm, DeLapp moved the Celts relentlessly with a well executed series of option plays combined with the hard-nosed running of Tom Leavitt.

Leavitt bulldozed through and twisted by Franklin defenders for 153 yards in a little more than three quarters of action, proving that his 200-yard effort against Crescent Valley the previous week was far from a fluke. DeLapp was instrumental in many of those gains, playing his role in the option offense to the hilt.

Pitch out or carry is the decision facing the quarterback on the option play, and DeLapp worked both attacks for consistent gainers.

But the offense did not do it on its own.

Coach Miller had high praise for the defensive unit, saying, "This was undoubtedly our best defensive effort of the year. Aside from Franklin's scoring drive in the first half, our defense controlled the field with a good, solid team effort. Our defensive coaches (Vic Backlund, Mike Jespersen, and John Wayland) deserve the credit for a fine job of preparation this week."

The game's first score came with 11:57 remaining in the first half as McNary drove 64 yards in ten plays for a touchdown.

Leavitt was the workhorse of the drive, carrying the ball six times for 34 yards. DeLapp started off the second quarter in fine form, as he snuck in from the one to culminate the drive.

Franklin scored next on a seventy yard drive made possible by a rather unorthodox offensive gainer.

A line drive punt by the Quaker kicker grazed the leg of a Celtic player downfield and Franklin recovered on McNary's 45-yard line. The Quakers seized this opportunity for a score, with Jack Goldhammer bulling in for the score nine plays later.

But that was the Quakers' swan song, as McNary tightened its grip on the game.

The Celtics took the following kickoff and drove 58 yards for a counter, the series highlighted by a Tom Leavitt scamper of 35 yards.

The turning point of the game occurred on the first play of the second half as Celt defender Tim Eaton picked off an errant pass and returned it to midfield. Though stifled at first, a fumbled punt turned the ball over to McNary and two Leavitt runs pushed the ball across the goal line.

Disaster struck quickly again for Franklin, as it fumbled the ball away on the next series of downs.

DeLapp wasted no time in making the turnover count, as he fired a 48-yard touchdown pass to Tim Eaton, who seemed to be in the right place at the right time all night long.

First Downs	Franklin	McNary
Rush Yds	7	14
Pass Yds	85	239
Tot Yds	66	76
Completions	151	314
Fumbles-Lost	5-23.3	3-11-1
Pens-Yds	4-3	3-2
Punts-Avg	2-35	6-60
	4-27.7	5-31.2

Franklin ...... 0 7 0 0 — 7
McNary ...... 0 14 21 0 — 35

Franklin: Goldhammer 2 run (Burk kick)
McNary: DeLapp 1 run (run failed); Leavitt 5 run (Harris run); Leavitt 5 run (DeLapp run); Eaton 48 pass from DeLapp (kick failed); Leavitt 5 run (Fox kick).

A football haze

Mist settled over the McNary football team Friday night, but the cold weather wasn't enough to stop the high-flying Celtics in a 35-7 win over Franklin. Mark DeLapp, reserve quarterback, paced the Celtic win. (For results of game, see Page 23) (Capital Journal Photo by Dan Poush)

MARK'S FOOTBALL CAREER

October 27, 1977, 1:22 PM

Hello,

I was sitting in Political Science class the other day, on the brink of falling asleep, trying to listen to the professor talk about ancient rulers and empires, etc. All of a sudden he's writing a couple of names on the board which ring a bell, Charles Martel and his grandson(?) Charlemagne (Charles the Great). I did manage to refrain from leaping out of my chair and exclaim, "I'm related to that guy! My grandmother's name was Martel. How do you like that?" I did however proclaim my heritage to couple of individuals afterward though. A mere fleeting moment of self-proclaimed glory.

But alas this was not to be the end. That night while catching up on some reading, I ran across the same, illustrious bloodline in a textbook in the library. The book was: Maxex, Chester C., Political Philosophies (Maximillan) 1948. And here is a copy of what my eyes beheld. Short, I must admit, but impressive just the same: "Emperor of the Romans." I can dig it! In fact, there's a copy of the page tacked to my bulletin board.

Well I just thought you (one day) would enjoy this little piece of historical fact, (how could they have missed it during "Bicentennial Minutes")? Maybe a copy aught to "anonymously" be sent to the papers...

Well that's enough for now—I've got to get to work on some less noteworthy material by some clown named Machiavelli.

Love,
Mark (Descendant of a Roman Emperor)

P.S. He named his son Nicholas Charlemagne DeLapp.

February 28, 1978
Mrs. Dawn Hill
Ban Office
Pacific Lutheran University

Dear Mrs. Hill,

The statement of February 27, 1978 sent by you has had the affect of leaving a very bad taste in my mouth. The last paragraph particularly disturbs me. Perhaps if you devoted more time to itemize your ambiguous statements rather than dwell so much on the threats, you would have more success and less correspondence. I realize your college isn't noted for its business academics but it does seem that anyone who works in the business office should have the presence of mind to just go over your bookkeeping and maybe just assume that you could be in error. Your letter of 1/13/78 states the total due PLU was $37.15 for which we sent you a check you cashed 2/3/78. In this statement you stated the interim board charge had been taken off the account (for which you had charged me without any cause). On 1/26/78 a statement with the credit and a $6.75 library charge was received. So your letter of today should have been an account of the money received and the balance of $6.75 which you had never included in any of the other statements. Mrs. Hill, I have paid over $6,000 to the Pac Lutheran University with the conviction that my son would receive the best in Christian education and I feel that I can afford to send him to any college he may choose but I don't feel the letter received from you was proper nor warranted. Your letter does convey the same attitude that my son said was very prevalent in the whole college atmosphere of PLU, perhaps the Christian philosophy needs to be reaffirmed.

P.S. After the second year, Mark transferred to University of Oregon in Eugene and got his degree, continuing on to Willamette University for his law degree.

IT GOES WITH THE TERRITORY

February 26, 1973

Mr. Fred H. Layman
Real Estate Commissioner
Real Estate Division
Dept. of Commerce

Dear Mr. Layman:

In response to your request for a complete written report on my action and reaction to the complaints received by your office concerning my subdivision known as Van Lyn, I hereby submit the following facts concerning these complaints and the complainants.

Van Lyn was the fulfillment of an idea that I had for several years of the need for modest, well built 2-bedroom homes, not pretentious, primarily for couples on fixed income who liked and wished for a new home but who did not like the heavy depreciation connected with the ownership of a mobile home, and who did not want government subsidy, but who did want a convenient location. I purchased 2 pieces of land with a total of 5 acres, less than two blocks to a shopping center for those who could not drive, on city sewer, water, bus line and developed it according to my concept of what the type of clientele would appreciate and built 21 homes simultaneously. It was my thought that by combining mass production with a minimum of finishing expenses, that the owners could do themselves (such as cleaning windows, landscaping, connecting own drain to downspouts) that I could sell 21 homes quickly with a very small profit margin on each one and everyone would benefit. I constructed 21 homes of similar architecture, with wall to wall carpet, built-in range, 13×18 living room, 13×15 master bedroom, birch cabinets, 14×26 attached garage, 12×12 patio with 6' sliding patio door, on a 6,000 ft. lot with streets, sidewalks, etc. No other builder was offering anything like this for within $2,000, for my total price which was $13,750.00.

My first buyer was a retired railroad pensioner with a service connected tax exemption who paid 20% down, assumed the 30 year mortgage, and has a payment of $75 per month! This was the type of person I had in mind, and has always been and is today the most satisfied homeowner you'll ever meet. Unfortunately, all buyers haven't been that happy and are the cause for the necessity of this letter.

In selling homes I tried to make it clear that the reason for being able to sell for this price was that if there were minor things that the buyer could do themselves, they would do them, but if there were any structural deficiencies that I would most certainly take care of them. This was my first development. Had I stuck rigidly to this policy and not tried to be Mr. Nice Builder, my problems may have been fewer, but instead I tried to please everyone. This has incurred aggravation, insult and defamation of character, from some individuals whom I know now could never be satisfied. One party in particular has been harassing me and fomenting dissatisfaction over very minor items. They are Mr. and Mrs. Jarvis at 4098 April Ct. They are a couple who purchased the home before being completed so they selected their carpeting, other floor covering, counter top, room color, plus the prime location They had a sale for their mobile home, and need possession on a certain date so we worked on their home specially to have it ready for their occupancy.

The first thing upon occupancy is she complained that the patio door glass had some scratches on it and I had no evidence that they did it, so I replaced it with a new one. She then made a list of small things that needed to be completed. I instructed my hired man to finish all the things on the list which he did with the exception of two things: 1) a molding 1 inch wide across the top of the kitchen cupboards was not stained, and 2) the attic access in the bedroom was a 2'×2' area where we had cut the ceiling. This needs a molding to cover the cut marks. These were so insignificant importance that we proceeded to finish the other homes where people were moving in. In the majority of cases, most buyers proceed on their own, as understood, to fix these small items but I did retain a man to finish anything that we felt should have been done in the normal course of construction.

In the fall I applied for a conditional use for the one remaining lot for a duplex (everyone had been advised beforehand that this lot was reserved for a duplex) and at the public hearing, Mr. Jarvis stood up and publicly declared that he objected because "DeLapp never finished any of the houses." I confronted him after the meeting to ask for an explanation of such a statement, whereupon he informed me that I hadn't fixed his moldings, and other people hadn't had their houses fixed, etc. I became a little angry and said that if he didn't like his unfinished house, that I would buy it from him for $15,000 to which he replied, "I could get $16,500," and I said, "You don't have a hell of a lot to complain about then." He made the statement then that, "I will cause you more damn trouble than you've ever seen. I'll even go down to that traders club meeting that you're the president of."

Since then, it has been one steady harassment including such ridiculous behavior as calling the sheriff when we did go to fix their molding. They called the county building inspector and both Mr. Dunigan and his superior went to look the house over and Mr. Dunigan informed me that a window in the bedroom had a factory defect in the installation of the glass. I immediately called the supplier who in turn called the manufacturer and upon offering to fix the window, was refused by the Jarvis' to let him, except on a Saturday when he doesn't work, although he could have done the job in 15 minutes while he was there.

You have received letters of complaint from other owners of homes, who Mr. Jarvis has agitated to write. Mr. and Mrs. Hurst live directly across the street: Mr. and Mrs. Hayford live directly East; Mr. and Mrs. Shaw live next to Hust and Mr. and Mrs. Peterson live directly north. He has also contacted Mr. and Mrs. Meyers who live down the street. He has approached everyone in the project and has been able to get only this much response. I have done the following:

Per request of Marion County Building Dept. we have: installed outside venting to the bathroom fans on all houses; installed a brace in the garage trusses from the outside wall to the inside wall; are in process now of checking all range vents.

Shaw: replaced electric outlet plug in garage; painted molding around back garage doors; fixed range vent that was overlooked in construction; framed attic access in garage.

Haford: installed drain through sidewalk for downspout drainage; repoured approach to driveway.

Peterson: stained and varnished portion of rear garage door; had electric company install extra outlet in bath; installed corner trim.

Jarvis: installed crawl space molding; stained and lacquered cabinet molding, attempted to fix window.

Muetze: cleaned and repainted overhang rafter where dirt had been painted over; installed connected range vent.

Mr. Muetze installed his own mailbox post which I offered to pay for.

Hoekstre: glued down metal conners; affixed crawl hole molding; replaced range vent pipe.

Hust: Mr. Hust made a list of deficiencies when they moved in and I personally took care that they were all complied with, all subsequent requests are not my responsibility.

Mrs. Hoekstre has been a continual source of irritation and has agreed to sell her home to me and is in escrow at this time. On the positive side, I think the remainder of the people in the area are quite well-satisfied. One party bought a second home after they had lived in theirs for a month; two instances of parents buying one home and children buying another; one couple was transferred and sold their homes immediately for $15,750 after having been there only 3 months. Some of the things which I did that were not required but I felt necessary was the installation of an 8" concrete drain tile to eliminate any possibility to a drainage problem to the property of Mr. Jarvis, Hayford, Wilson and Sikinger. I allowed the owner to use lumber that was excess and piled on the vacant lot (which Mr. Jarvais, Hust, Hayford, Peterson and Muetze were the biggest users) one built a double decked work bench the full length of his garage).

I have tried to conduct my business in an honest a forthright manner. Never have I promised anything that I later denied. I think my reputation is above reproach and I intend to keep it that way.

SILVER ANNIVERSARY OF BEING A BROKER
1985

*In writing this in 1985, I really had no idea of being in the
business for another 25 years, really outliving my contem-
poraries. Printed by the "Salem Realtor" monthly paper.*

In 1960 I started selling real estate, but that is a misnomer.
No one sells real estate—people buy real estate—we just
show them what and how they can buy. After two years
of working and observing how easy fellows such as Lee
Ohmart, George Grabenhorst, and the Rawlins boys were
getting rich, I decided I could do the same. So 25 years ago
on Columbus Day while everyone's roof and trees were
blowing away, I was ecstatic. I had received the notice that I
had passed the Real Estate Brokers exam and the world was
given what it desperately needed—another real estate office.
It took many days of heavy thought and concentration and
examining of clever names and ideas until it dawned on me
the name to use—DeLapp Real Estate.

The 25 years have gone by quickly. I've done selling,
buying, developing, trading, borrowing, talking, yelling,
and crying. I've raised rents, kids and hell. I've had two
wives and 20 cars. I've built new, fixed old and done a lot
of painting on the in-between. I've owned property from
North Howell to North Minnesota and from South Salem
to Southern Oregon. I've farmed, fooled, fished and fiddled
around. I raised three kids and two of them turned out
good, the other one became a lawyer.

Through all the 25 years I have never considered changing professions—I never got rich but I have outlasted most
of my peers. I did a few things right and a lot of things

wrong, but as Frank says, "I did it my way." In this quarter years century, I have become friends to a lot of really good people and a few not so good. I hope to use this format in a series to thank you for your support—so, every 25 years you can expect to read my follow-up report. But through it all I never quite am finished. There's more to do. My dues are paid another year.

MY FOOT IN THE DOOR

My inaugural open letter to motel owners on the coast and other destination points, 1985.

Dear Sir:

The business climate of Oregon is perceived by investors and business operators to be on the rise. We in Oregon are in the enviable position of having a good tourist business, low costs, and comparatively low real estate values—this looks good to our out-of-state residents who are experiencing high costs, polluted, crowded environments, and high original investments values.

This is the reason I am writing you. After 25 years in the real estate profession, most of which have been in the investment and exchanging field, I feel the time is right for a concentrated effort selling good motel and allied businesses, i.e. restaurants, lounges, RV parks, marinas, etc. No other business I know of has the state paying the advertising and seeking business like the motel business has. They finally recognize the value of tourists, and that fact sounds alluring to the out-of-state operator. Every indication is that the next 2 years is the time of opportunity and as an operator now, if you have the idea of selling, the time to sell is when you have a buyer.

Although the big motels are marketable to the investment type buyer, it's my feeling that the small quality motel that can be operated by a couple who have always wanted to own their own business, is always saleable with substantial down payments and a realistic expectation.

I will not try to extol my capabilities here, but if you are thinking of selling, I would welcome the opportunity to meet you face to face. I will have no more than five good properties at any one time and will donate my whole time to your property. My contacts are many. My reputation is my best recommendation. My know-how is based on 25 years of successful real estate business.

Give me a call—let's talk.

Sincerely,
Dave DeLapp

WHO ARE WE?
SALEM CREATIVE MARKETING CLUB

*A memo to listing clients and prospects, 1985. Printed in
the Salem Realtor monthly bulletin.*

Over 35 years ago a group of enterprising realtors in Salem started meeting every Wednesday morning for breakfast and to exchange information on the properties they had listed and whom
they thought may exchange for other property that was also for
sale. This format has been successful for 35 years without inter-
ruption—through bad times and good. That old "Traders Club"
has evolved into today's Creative Marketing Club. The reason
for the name change was to protect the complete involvement
of the members. We still meet every Wednesday morning. The
whole purpose is Broker Cooperation in marketing your property and discussing the events of outside forces that affect your
ownership of real estate.

In addition to our weekly marketing program, we invite
those people who are knowledgeable in what is happening
in the government controls, taxes, DEQ, LCDC, legislature,
etc. These people all have a vital effect on the marketability of
your property, and as your counselor and agent we intent to
be informed—at least enough to wave the red flag. We also
participate in quarterly meetings with other similar motivated clubs located throughout Oregon, Washington and California to give exposure to other cooperating members who
take the extra time every week to keep informed. We expose
your listings to other brokers and present your needs to par-
ticipating brokers from Salem, Canby, Albany, Corvallis,
Stayton, Monmouth, and many guests each week from other
clubs. When you see, "Member, Salem Creative Marketing
Club," you will know this person is working for YOU.

ON ORGANIZING THE
INDEPENDENT BROKERS CO-OP
Sent to the small broker

When Multiple Listing Broker (MLB) started, no one had any idea the ultimate significance it would impact on our real estate business—that today we would grow to be operating on an annual budget of over one-half million dollars in the bank. When the Realtors was formed, it was based on an idea to bring a standard of ethics to an industry that that had none. I'm sure no one had any conception that it would be a national force with powerful input into Washington on every issue that affects property ownership. My point: I believe the concepts we ponder and kick around here can grow to be a force in the industry whose ultimate importance cannot be ignored. We must do this with all the intelligence and forethought at our disposal. The emergence of large real estate companies backed by big money is merely the recognition by an organizer that there is strength and savings in volume marketing and he did it for a profit, knowing that there are people who will pay a part of what they earn to participate in such an organization. We are here with the idea that by organizing, we can affect savings instead of cost and provide a better service in doing so.

We can't legislate against human nature. Golden rule didn't say do unto other or God will break your kneecaps. Fair participation in the organization is a voluntary personal thing. Even though always some member will try to stretch the rules and exceed the limits. A clear recognition of what's good for all will maintain the strength and good of our union.

We are smart enough, if we all contribute, to set forth the right covenants and restrictions to make this a lasting union. Our concept is right, the time is right, our integrity must be right.

This can be the Genesis of a new force in the real estate industry—an alliance of experienced brokers advocating controlled service by those licensed to do so, and by those who know their business. We must keep in mind that how well we succeed will be viewed not only by the big competing companies, but by the public as well. We always have one thing going for us—everyone is rooting for the little man.

Non-franchised brokers form real estate group

Salem real estate broker **Dave DeLapp** has announced the formation of Independent Cooperating Brokers, an association of non-franchised real estate brokers in Marion and Polk counties.

More than 25 brokers have joined so far. said DeLapp, the association's founder.

Through the association, the brokers will collectively promote and advertise real estate, but will continue to operate their own real estate businesses independently. The brokers also will maintain their individual memberships with the multiple listing service and Realtor organizations. More information is available from DeLapp at 364-0077.

THE INDEPENDENT BROKER –
THE ADVANTAGE OF EXPERIENCE
Publication to introduce my newly created organization.

We all know in our industry from the standpoint of customer relations and satisfactory service, that bigger is not necessarily better. In fact, we all know that it is indeed NOT nearly as good. When dealing with the most valuable possession most people ever have the ownership of real estate, the more knowledge, the more experience, the more common sense we impart, the better off everyone is. Yet today the efficient, knowledgeable broker in the Salem area (and everywhere else) is being out-maneuvered and out-advertised by a few large organizations who advertise and play on the same theme that bigger IS better. We small and independent brokers are relegated to fighting over the leftovers, simply because we ARE independent. In my book, independence is a virtue—it should be exploited and made known to the public the benefits that they have by dealing with the small personal broker, and I mean the broker in small offices in this case. This is the basis of the Independent Brokers Association.

IBA was formed to derive the benefits of volume rates on advertising and to share our concerns that affect the public. By using this cooperative format, we give the same personal service and the benefits of experience, yet also have the resources to advertise at reduced rates.

It's human nature to want to be associated with success, and success today is correlated with big: Big autos, big houses, big drinks (32 ounces to a gulp). So what intrigues the first time seller or buyer? "150 sales people doing millions of dollars of business each month," when in reality there are a lot of loose canons out there with very little supervision from any experienced broker. There are literally hundreds of new licensees every year going into the real estate profession and someone has to be the first clients. Who do you want: a doctor doing his first operation? A lawyer facing his first judge? A mechanic with a manual in one hand? A real estate salesman with a new license? Members of the IBA offers hundreds of years of experience and each Broker personally reviews your needs.

In the most important decision of one's life, it is important not to mistake quantity for quality. The small independent broker recognizes quality makes for repeat business, and he works hard for that business. The client is the beneficiary.

The best example of cooperating being a benefit is the Multiple Listing Service (MLB). Forty years ago all the offices were small and cutthroat. MLB was started "to level the playing field" for all offices—thus giving the one man office access to all the listings and enabling him to give the same service to his clients as the larger offices offer. MLB has been extremely successful and both the brokers and clients have benefited.

The concept of small broker affiliation has been done very effectively by the insurance industry and many independent insurance companies today represent many large underwriters, and we are better served by them.

There are approximately 175 offices in the Salem area that have experienced brokers with less than 10 sales persons. For the person who needs that good judgment, and has proved his success by his longevity in the business, the small independent broker warrants consideration.

ON GETTING HIS LAW DEGREE
FROM WILLAMETTE UNIVERSITY, 1985

Mark,

My cup runneth over. My pride can hardly be contained. You have again achieved yet another goal. You have reached a beginning. The pinnacle you now rest on only raises you above the plateau and enables you to have an unobstructed view of the higher mountains—taller pinnacles—heights and goals that were before only a dream. You have, ever since you were a kid, a dedication to achievement and an ability to attain- a perception of your own self that I have believed in and trusted. Even though your goals and your ability to obtain these goals have been greater than mine ever were, I have never doubted that ability. You have made these aspirations seem so logical and attainable, that I have just accepted them and perhaps expected you to do them and even more. If my assumed expectations have added to your determinations, then maybe those expectations were valid.

The odd results of success is that it is never final. Reaching a goal only unfolds a myriad of other worlds and visions that were not viewable before. You can't see the higher mountains until you reach the peak of the one you're climbing and a climber never quits. He rests on his laurels to savor the view for a while, but there's always a loftier height, another pinnacle, a little higher all arising from a level above the level of complacency and mediocre achievements. After you reach the first peak, the next one is easier. Your confidence is greater, the thrill of achievement, though no less, and the known quantity and the satisfaction can be a way of life. Every dad I'm sure has a gnawing apprehension when his kids embark on a course that he knows is hard and takes guts to stick to because he's afraid "they will not stay the course" and will settle for less. Maybe now, I can rest assured that when Mark sets his goal, I can be assured he will reach it. But, I probably always will believe you can achieve more. That you are an achiever. That there are only the limits of your own ambitions to keep you from being an extraordinary achiever. In your growing up, I have become wiser, and yet, I probably never fully grasped the extent of your accomplishment capabilities, but you persevered in spite of it.

I am so proud of you now, that I feel ashamed that I let you irritate me. But, that will happen again, so bear with me. These are my thoughts, you owed me nothing and yet I feel rewarded. I take a personal satisfaction and even give myself credit for having some part of your happiness. What you do, good or bad, feel joy or sad, your dad is proud of you today and your dad was proud of you yesterday. I expect to be proud of you in the future.

Dad.

REAL ESTATE
LAW FIRM
MARK L.
DELAPP, P.C.

A law practice limited to
real property transactions
and construction
contract disputes

"Mark DeLapp's firm has represented our company in both transactions and litigation. His in-depth and yet common sense legal expertise has been a great asset to our business."

Joe Lyons, Co-Owner
JDL Development, Portland, OR

The Law Office of
Mark L. DeLapp, P.C.

Plaza 125
12746 S.E. Stark
Portland, OR 97233, 503-257-6050

"Our business is representing the best interest of your business."

ROXANNE

My ideas come in momentary, questionable flashes of brilliance and so it was with Roxanne. I had bought this neat little 13-acre farm with a nice house and very good out buildings, one of which was a barn with pens and a fenced small pasture originally for a horse barn but equally adaptable for any other type of animal. Hence came the brilliant flash— why not a pig? So the first act was buy two weaners—one red, one black, Pinky and Inky—whose fate was predetermined by being eunuchs, to grow up as hogs. They were nice, they were friendly, and they were delicious. They also were the idea of begetting the future hog farm (on a minor scale). I knew something about swine—we had grown Hampshires in our early years and taken grand champion for brood sows at State Fair—so I decided that was the place to buy the best hog in the state, and I did. The 4-H Grand Champion Hampshire bred gilt with registration papers denoting lineage of champions but with the strip-tease name, Roxanne. This auction was to benefit the education of some farm kid who had raised her; I didn't intend sending him to Harvard, but with the bidding done, Roxanne was all mine and a farm kid with hog manure on his shoes was smiling ear to ear.

God made the Hampshire breed black but with the concession to some racial equality put a white belt around front quarters making the Hamp a very distinguished breed. Roxanne had met another Hamp who she may have thought was a bore but too late found out he was a boar, so she was in a family way when I took her to her new home. She adapted to the new home very well. Having been raised in a big family, she was one contented young gilt with warm dry bed, nice open pasture to root and run, and an owner who rubbed her belly every day and fed her apples and corn along with her grain. Roxanne was a female who never had to watch her weight, and grow she did, and even though she was eating for eight or ten she was sylish, but not neat.

Her first personal act of self-satisfaction was to root out, using her tough snout, a long trench in the dirt which, when filled with rain, made one hog-heaven mud hole. Although this idyllic life suited Roxanne, she was rapidly approaching motherhood. It only takes 4 months to make piglets so having had her for less than 3 months, the maternity room was made ready and one late November night, she had eight pretty little black-and-white fat cute pigs. Roxanne was a good mother, and like any mother, thought they were special. Although she weighed 350 pounds, she was very careful in lying down, making sure no little pig was under her. Although a single mother, she raised eight strong, healthy purebred children that I was able to sell for breeding stock to the next 4-H entrepreneur.

Now the problem arose as to how to find a boyfriend for Roxanne. Because it's not financially feasible to keep a boar fed and bedded for just one sow, I had to start pimping for a pig for a one night stand. Not living in an area of a lot of hog farms, it became a challenge, until I picked up a hog magazine of purebred Hampshire hog farms, with only one small problem: they were in Iowa and Roxanne was in Oregon. The solution: artificial insemination. I not only was a pimp for a pig, I was also to become a pig (fornicator). About a month after weaning her brood, this now 600 pound perfect picture of a swine pulcitrude was smiling and making little noises—she was looking for love.

The semen and "device" was air mailed in a sealed cooler with Penthouse-type instructions on how to proceed. The device was a plastic replica of the business part of a male pig, which to those unfamiliar with the that anatomy, is shaped to make no mistake where the term *screw* comes from. She was willing and, it being my first time, I was nervous, but following instructions, I did the deed and could only wait 28 days to see if she had conceived. She didn't.

That didn't work, so now it's finding a boar to do it right. Thus began the series of courtships; each time she needed companionship, we loaded her into the pickup and hauled her all over the country to her boyfriends. We drew no racial boundaries—one litter was red, one black-and-white, one black—but she loved them all and seemed to enjoy the travel. Of course you have heard the story of the farmer who hauled her to the neighbor in a wheelbarrow and brought her home and the next morning she was lying in the wheelbarrow ready to go—I swear Roxanne got easier to load every time. It was on one of those Roxanne romantic romps to a community college on the coast that had a scales that Roxanne weighed in at over 800 pounds. My little girl was growing up. I'm sure that when pregnant and fat, she tipped the scales at 1,000 pounds. She became the showpiece of the farm, including for the mayor of Salem who had breakfast with us. And anyone else who would ever visit us would ask, "Do you still have Roxanne?"

The final chapter came when I got seriously injured picking corn for her and her family. I was forced to sell all my animals which I did with no great remorse, with the exception of Roxanne. She was my big 'ole fat friend and a beautiful animal. I sold her to a family, but I reserved visitation rights. I was satisfied she went to a good home.

ROXANNE AND FAMILY

4

THE ACCIDENT

THE LIFE CHANGER

I suppose every significant event starts on a seemingly ordinary day. And Saturday, April 6, 1986 started out as one of them, with no warning of what was to come, but it was the most significant happening of my 87 years. It was one of those beautiful, warm spring days in Oregon and I had come out to the farm. It was a day God had intended for no one to die, and He included me.

My farm was a semi-isolated 55-acre property of the finest prairie land, ten miles from my home. That day, with the sun in my eyes, I decided to harvest a small field of "field corn," or corn that hasn't been harvested in the Fall (with my boys grown and gone, things didn't always get done in time). This was my weekend recreation and I looked forward to it. I often went out there by myself to plow, plant, or pick.

Today I would pick, and I elected to do this task with an old one-row Woods Brothers field corn picker. Now, you must understand the working of the machine to fully comprehend what happened that day. This was a "Rube Goldberg" machine: a perfectly engineered combination of chains, gears, rollers, and shafts pulled behind a tractor with a power shaft, that gathers, husks, and drops pretty yellow dried corn into a wagon. Going down a row of corn, the machine strips the ear of corn from the stalk and drops it into two rapidly revolving rollers, not unlike the wringer on an old washing machine. The rollers are each about 36 inches long, and made of hard, serrated rubber. As they rub together these rollers grab the dry husks and bare the corn, drop it onto the elevator and then deposit into the wagon. Understanding the working of a machine doesn't necessarily mean that even a well-seasoned farmer couldn't forget to be careful, and I forgot to be careful.

I spent a pleasant afternoon picking all but the last one-half row of corn when my problems began. The small drive chain at the bottom of the elevator broke and fell off. I attempted to find it, but with only 100 yards to complete my work, I decided to just stop every few feet when the corn piled up, sweep it into the chain elevator with my arm and be done with it. It was a good plan, except for reaching in to pick up an ear lodged in the flaying roller.

Now these rollers are designed to grab anything they come into contact with. In one split second, they grabbed my right hand fingers and instinctively I reached and grabbed them with my left hand. I was caught, with both hands in the picker. I screamed in pain as the rollers kept turning at 200 RPM, tearing skin and bone off my hands; crushing and grinding my fingers, except my thumbs and little finger. In stark terror, I hollered for help, I cried and I prayed but soon I realized that no one would be able to hear me. To top it off, this picker that had my hands in its jaws was powered by a tractor hitched eight feet away with enough gas to continue running for another five hours. I was in a life and death situation, completely and utterly alone.

A lot of people have tried to describe terror, but until you have faced the circumstance of possible death alone, you cannot fully comprehend the hopelessness and helplessness. Facing dying alone is as lonely as it gets. When a person realizes this, the brain doesn't shut down. Instead, my mind began running through the calculations: I am ten miles from my wife who wasn't expecting me home until dark—another four hours—and a half-mile away from the nearest neighbor. As those rollers continued to spin, my mind reeled with questions: What do I do? What about going into shock? Will I pass out? How much of this pain can I take? Will I bleed to death? Can I kick the chain off? No way.

But can I work my right hand down towards the end of the rollers? Yes. I began working it down and there was room to free it one finger at a time and I thought, "YES! My right hand is free with a good thumb and an unbroken little finger." One hand is free.

"I AM HALFWAY OUT!" But that's like saying I'm drowning in eight feet of water instead of 16. With all the strength in me, I grabbed my left wrist and tried to pull. No good. My heavy wedding band had gone behind the whirring rollers and would not come out or let me move that hand down the rollers. Trapped like a wild animal in a trap that chews his leg off to escape, it seems ridiculous to be in that tragic position and to now think about being lucky, but my mind could only think of one act. I know that if I had had a knife in my pocket, I would have tried to cut off that ring finger, with bleeding to death as the result.

In my hip pocket was a pair of side cutter pliers. With my good thumb and little finger, I got them out with the thought of cutting off that ring finger. Of course, it was underneath those big rollers still ready to suck in anything else it could grab so I discarded that idea. Instead, I reasoned to stick the pliers between the rollers near my hand and spread the rollers or stop the machine. When inserting the pliers, they went between the rollers and instantly fell to the ground underneath and were irretrievable. But that was the right idea—some way to stuff something between the rollers. My salvation then occurred to me. I raised my foot up onto the frame and I took off my 6″ high leather shoe. With the very clear awareness that this was my only chance, I stuffed that shoe, top first, between the rollers. The slip clutch began clattering, the machine stopped and it spread the two rollers apart—allowing me to pull out my hand and mangled fingers. I was free! No one was going to come out hours later and find me dead in a damned old machine grinding away all my flesh and bones. No way can I express the relief, the joy, the just plain thankfulness that I felt as I stood there with both hands; bloody pieces of meat, but I was free. I had beaten it, but now I needed to find help.

I backed away, I had done it. From here on, I've got it made! I'm alive! But throughout all this, I kept thinking just how much pain and how much shock can a body endure. So when I turned to walk the half mile to my pickup I wasn't sure I could make it so I stopped, went back to the tractor and got on. Knowing I'd have to drive to the nearest neighbor I attempted to unhook the corn picker. Another mistake. I'd have to take the pin out of the power to take off the shaft to get it unhooked. But luck was with me and it came out easy. I drove with my elbows to my pick up and drove onwards to the neighbors. In my euphoria of escape I never thought of anything else but to get to the hospital and let the doctor fix me. Little idea did I have that I would come closer yet to dying than in the darned picker.

In escaping one horrible experience, it never occured to me that more could happen. I drove to the neighbor, laid on the horn till she came out. I had to have her open the door and said, "You have got to take me the hospital." Seeing my mangled hands, she immediately gave her boyfriend instructions to call the hospital and my wife, after wrapping my hands in a towel. He was not the pick of the litter as the first word out of his mouth was, "I never drove a pickup before." I said, "It's an automatic, just go." So we did, at 20 miles an hour. He replied, I don't know Salem, I know the hospital in Silverton." So we headed to the country hospital instead of the big city hospital.

To this day I remember it was the longest frantic 30 minutes I've ever spent. We stopped at every stop sign, waited for all the traffic, stopping and starting, with no sense of emergency at all. The pain in my hands was beginning to be unbearable. He even had to be told to go to the Emergency Entrance, not the front door. And of course, they didn't know I was coming, my neighbor Laura had called the Salem Hospital. The nurses did give me a shot for my pain and cleaned my hands a bit, then put me in an ambulance and took me into Salem, another 30 miles . The pain dulled, and I was able to let go of control and let the doctor take over. My wife was waiting at the hospital and was absolutely shocked to see both my hands wrapped in bandages. I said to her, "Honey, I really screwed up my hands." I was taken straight to the operating room.

The next morning the doctor told me what the operation had entailed. He had to amputate four fingers and thought he had salvaged two more, that he wasn't too sure of. He also said that it had taken him six and half hours to clean up the damage, and that he had done the best he could to clean out all the ground in dirt from the wounds. Then he said that the next morning he would unwrap it and figure out what to do next. I was relieved to be out of immediate danger, I had dodged a bullet, but now it was the problem of getting well. As I lay there, I contemplated the damage that was done and how it could affect the rest of my life, not even knowing of the complications to come. I thought I was in good hands.

The following day the surgeon made his rounds and told me that he had made the decision not to unwrap my hands and instead to send me to an orthopedic surgeon in Portland who specialized in hand surgery. This surgeon assured me that I would be just fine until this other surgeon could see me.

My wife drove me to the Portland hospital and we were there before noon. The doctor we were assigned to see was returning from vacation and I wouldn't be available until the next morning. My hands were beginning to smell rotten.

I was assigned to a 2-bed ward with a male nurse. Now, as a small time farmer I had smelled animal wounds, and knew the smell of decaying and rotten flesh, so I told the male nurse who was attending me, "I need a doctor, now." He agreed, and although his shift ended at 3 p.m. he spent the remainder of the afternoon trying to find a doctor to come to my room and look at my hands. A woman doctor arrived and although the smell was very noticeable and my temperature had raised and she said that she wouldn't remove the bandage and that the doctor would take care of it in the morning. I remember very little of that night or being taken to the operating room the next morning. By then gas gangrene had set in and he had to remove all the fingers on my left hand except my thumb, back to the knuckles. He immediately sent me to Providence Hospital where the only hyperbaric machine in town was available. He said that it would saturate my body with oxygen and kill the bacteria that made my hands smell so badly by virtue of the fact that 100% oxygen kills bacteria.

When we arrived at that Providence, they were expecting me. However, there was something missing, or rather someone—the technician who was needed to run the specialized piece of machinery. The doctor, when he inquired where this technician was, was told that they could not get a hold of him by phone, and that it was ringing busy. He angrily told the person in charge to call the state police and to get the person and bring him in now, because as he said, "We have a dying man here waiting." That was when I realized how near I was to losing my life. It seems that after the awful struggle I had to free myself from that dreaded corn picker, getting myself into one hospital after another, and still waited for the surgeon.

Now, it turns out that the technician had taken his phone off the hook. As soon as he arrived I was finally put into the hyperbaric machine that was to finally save my life. A hyperbaric machine is a glass cylinder three feet in diameter that is like being buried alive. It was then I said, "I fought to save my life to get here, and when the people who could help me the most became available, they damn near killed me. I was put into the 100% pure O^2 tube for two hours a day for five days. Definitely not for the claustrophobic. They also soaked my hands in an iodine whirlpool bath to get rid of all the dead tissue which was extremely painful, but they gave me excellent care. Finally, the best orthopedic hand surgeon in the city grafted skin back on both hands with skin from my thigh, he saved my thumbs and saved my badly damaged forefinger on my right hand.

This enabled me weeks later to be able to write and feed myself and continue my real estate occupation. After the left hand healed with only a thumb left, we devised the prosthesis that I advised the orthopedist to design so that I could hold a fishing pole and not a shovel handle. With only one hand, I was able to do farming to some extent—but I never picked another ear of corn.

As a life-changer this traumatic escape changed the goal line. At 57 it immediately moved from 50 yards away to ten yards. My retirement age moved up. It became reality that if I'm going to play, I had to get into the game. Accomplishment at work isn't the whole story of life. I now had only two thumbs and two fingers. I could no longer catch a ewe to trim her feet. I could no longer be my own mechanic. Or pick up a sack of grain. I had made a good living with my limited brain power and that could continue unimpaired, but I was suddenly made aware the time to live is now. There is no guarantee of the future. So, again I've been lucky. I've lived 31 more years, travelled in my motor home, fished Alaska, crossed the country to the east coast, gone to Mexico, Costa Rica, Italy, England. I saw my kids succeed and grandkids grow up. I developed more projects and built my home on the river. Maybe I would have done this without the accident, but maybe I would have said, "There's always tomorrow." It taught me that there may not be.

A SENSE FOR HUMOR

The doctor had worked six and a half hours preparing my mangled fingers and so when he came into my hospital room the next morning he looked very worried as to my mental condition, with both hands suffering extreme damage. Having amputated several fingers it was very evident he was concerned. I said, "Doc, am I going to be able to play the piano?" With extreme agitation he replied, "I'm afraid not." "Well, don't let it bother you," I said, "I couldn't before." He laughed: "I was about to say 'Not unless you play with your toes.'" "Well how about someone writing a concerto for two thumbs and a little finger?" I suggested.

Humor has two senses: One is a sense *of* humor and the other is a sense *for* humor. Will Rogers had a sense of humor and did more for national morale during the depression than any politician, including the president, ever could, because his sense of the time for humor was right. We might have been hungry, but we laughed.

It was said that Roosevelt won the election in 1940 when he couldn't shake this perception of being an elitist; born wealthy, having never worked a day in his life. There was a war starting and he was running for a third term when he was criticized very heavily for sending a plane to pick up his dog. He said, "I can take a personal attack but when they start picking on Fala they have gone too far." He was reelected an unprecedented third term. Bob Dole commented the next morning after losing his election, "I slept like a baby: I woke up every hour and cried."

So what is this sense of humor? No other animal on this earth has the ability to laugh or cry. When you touch something hot, you don't think but your sense of feeling prevents burning. Something smells bad, you don't think, instead, you leave it alone. Something tastes bad, your senses say, "don't swallow." This sense of humor or a sense for humor is a method to get someone to accept you, because after all, how can someone dislike you if you can make them laugh? It can be a warning to the brain if you can't laugh, you've got a problem and be careful of those who can't. It's a built-in release for an overloaded mind. The very joy of living needs needs to be expressed. Why do we think we endear ourselves to someone if we can make them laugh. Yes, our best friends can cry with this us, but more often they laugh with us. I guess the joke is on us. We are born and we are given this great blessing of laughing because God knows we are here for just a short time. This great gift of laughter was given to us to make this short life enjoyable, knowing there is an end.

5

ON THE BACKSTRETCH

CONFLICT OF POLITICS

Just soon after being elected, Governor Schaub proposed
adding two additions to the capitol building.

E very governor has done something which he can be re-membered for. Hatfield's government: re-organization; McCall: the Bottle Bill and now Governor Schaub makes a bid for posterity by putting wings on the Capitol. Even with all the power we recognize as emanating from the Capitol, he'll never get it off the ground. Those who criticize this dubious expenditure of $10 million dollars offered the suggestion that the money might be better spent on penitentiary facilities to alleviate the over-crowded and premature release of non-rehabiliated prisoners. This conflict of ideologies, i.e. capital wings versus prisoner rehabilitation, has an apparent incomprehensible difference that precludes solution. Not so. Inherent in these two problems is a common solution. It can be implemented with benefits for both. It is this simple: Take the excess prisoners and lock them up in the new wings. Let them become the lawmakers. This program has several advantages. One, it would restore public confidence. We would know for sure who the liars, crooks, cheats were and where they were. Two, and most important: After they deliberated, and enacted their programs, if they passed any such bills such as 10-26, the Criminal Disclosure Act or SB-100, we would be sure they were not ready for release, that they still held a grudge against the general public and they had not been adequately rehabilitated to think in normal terms. Our recourse could then be to send them back to the main facilities or, hold them over for another term.

GOVERNMENT INVOLVEMENT IN PUBLIC HOUSING
Used as a carrot for a vote

Emerson said, "He dwells nowhere that dwells everywhere." I think we will certainly agree that the home owners of this nation or of any nation have been the dependable element of the populace. I am whole-heartedly in favor of home owner-ship. I have based my livelihood and dedication to this prin-ciple. But this privilege, and it is a privilege and not a right, should be earned to be an effective instrument of individual freedom and not given by the government in a socialistic way.

When property ownership is earned by the owner, he be-comes the backbone of the nation. Property owners simply do not riot—they simply do not demonstrate—they simply and effectively pay the way for education, fire departments, and playgrounds. When not earned; when given property by the government (using your tax money and mine), we perpetuate the thought of "the world owes me the same that everyone else has, whether I produce my share or not."

I don't mean to be misunderstood about the govern-ment participation in public housing. The Federal Housing Administration was created in June 1934, and this organi-zation has helped millions since then, but in this way: Our Federal government has said to private lending institutions such as banks and insurance companies, "If you will make low down payment mortgages to borrowers, we approve, on property we inspect and at the interest rate we prescribe, that we will guarantee this amount in case you have to fore-close." Now keep in mind that at this time, the government is not giving anything to anybody, it is merely backing up the loaning agency, and neither has any compensation from the government. However, you say, sure, but when the borrower defaults, what happens? Every month, his regular payment and extra 1/2 percent of the amount borrowed goes into a reserve fund used to bail out the delinquencies, so it does not cost us a cent.

There are other fine programs administered in much the same way, such as Farm Home Administration, which makes low interest loans to farmers, or the Federal GI agencies who guarantee loans much the same same as FHA with a lower down payment provision and without the 1/2 percent extra for the reserve: Simply rewarding the veteran who gave a portion of his lifetime to the preservation of this country. We must not also forget to mention one of the most successful programs ever inaugurated in the United States and that is the state of Oregon Veteran Loan Program, which has always paid its own way with great benefits to those who earn it at a lower rate. There is nothing wrong with helping when someone needs it, but as recent years have demonstrated, giving to the undeserved may lead to more political votes, and we all lose in the end.

ESSAY ON GOVERNMENT DEVELOPMENT

Written for the monthly Realtors newsletter 35 years ago

In any direct government project, never have they proved that they can do it economically and this includes fighting wars or landing on the moon. Sometimes it's necessary from the standpoint of being the only means to coordinate separate industries, but you and I pay through the nose. In the case of housing, it's unnecessary. The bids on the turnkey projects are running 15 to 20% higher than comparable housing on the private market. The cost of each unit of the Eola Retirement Village, being just one bedroom, concrete floored, with cement block walls, was more than private builders are providing 3 bedroom homes for on individual lots. Every time Uncle Sugar gets into it directly, you and I get it in the neck.

Plans have been submitted to the government for cleaning up slum areas in the east whereby private enterprise would rejuvenate areas if given tax benefits for the expense, but these plans have been rejected in favor of completely destroying the old and relocating the residents, creating a shortage of housing by their very own design.

We are becoming a society of believing in the elusive premise of something for nothing. We are slowly giving up our independence for government controlled security. When we give up that last bulwark of independence, the sole ownership of property, we have lost the battle of the individual, and we will have become government controlled. To take care of the old and the lame is the duty of us all—to help those who will not help themselves is destroying our democratic way of life. You and I must remain steadfast in our belief in independent action or that something for nothing will be reversed—nothing for something—our freedom and independence.

SOMETIMES WE WIN

Real Estate Agency
158 12th Street
Salem, OR 97301

Attn: Steve Haws

Dear Sir:

I recently filed a complaint against a Mr. DeLapp with
DeLapp Real Estate. The problem has been completely
solved and I have been misrepresented on the matter. Mr.
DeLapp is not at all at fault. So I hope you will withdraw the
complaint made against Mr. DeLapp. Furthermore, I would
like to thank you for taking the time in this matter, and I
would like to apologize for any inconveniene, I may have
caused your office. Again, I would like to thank you very
much in this matter. So, if you may, I would like it very much
if you could please close the file you have open against Mr.
DeLapp or DeLapp Real Estate office.

Thank you,
Patricia S. Munz
2035 Kennedy Circle N.E.
Salem, OR 97303

MOST PEOPLE ARE GOOD

July 26th, 1988

Dear Dave,

Enclosed you'll find the copy of the letter I sent to "the real estate agency." I mailed that out today so that they would get it by Thursday. Again, I apologize for all the inconvenience that this has caused. Also, I myself should have sent it to you in the first place instead of listening to everyone else's gossip about how if I did not get myself an attorney, I would lose the furniture and everything. If I had went to you in the first place, instead of listening to my mother, it would have saved us a lot of trouble in the long run. Again, I am sorry about all the trouble and I appreciate everything.

Thank you,
Patricia S. Munz

FIRST FIRING FORT SUMPTER CIVIL WAR IN WRITING

GATTI, GATTI, MAIER AND ASSOCIATES
ATTORNEYS AT LAW

April 9, 1990
Certified Mail

David DeLapp
858 Commercial Street, SE
Salem, OR 97301

Re: Darrin K. Henderson

Dear Mr. DeLapp:

Please be advised that our offices have been retained by Darrin K. Henderson to take over representation of his claim for injuries arising from the collapsing bathroom floor of the apartment he resided in. Mr. Henderson's injuries are quite serious and he has been unable to work. I would appreciate someone contacting me from your insurance carrier immediately.

In addition, I would appreciate receiving all the documentation showing the reason for evicting Darrin, Sarah, and their newborn baby following the accident. I would also like verification and reasons why you chose to evict Sarah Henderson's mother who lives in the same complex. I would remind you that the Oregon Landlord-Tenant Statutes provide for sanctions and treble damages where persons who file complaints regarding the condition of their premises are unreasonably evicted. I look forward to hearing from you shortly.

Best Regards,
Kathryn E. Jackson

146

FRAUD AND EXTORTION

The Law Office of Mark L. DeLapp

April 24, 1990

RE: Kathryn E. Jackson
Gatti, Gatti, Maier and Associates
1761 Liberty Street SE
Salem, OR 97302

Re: Darrin Henderson

Dear Ms. Jackson:

David DeLapp of DeLapp Real Estate has forwarded me a copy of your April 9, 1990 letter regarding Mr. Henderson.

Please be advised that Mr. Henderson was never injured on the premises within the apartment that he once resided in. At no time did any bathroom floor collapse nor was there any defective condition regarding the bathroom in his apartment. In fact, Mr. Henderson appeared to be quite able-bodied as he removed personal effects from the apartment subsequent to him being evicted. Mr. Henderson apparently retained the services of somebody who represented himself as an investigator who took pictures of the apartment and bathroom floor. I would suggest you take a look at these photographs.

Darrin, Sarah and "the newborn baby" were properly and legally evicted by order of the court. If they had any defenses to that FED action, I am sure they knew how to obtain free legal services in which to prosecute those defenses. In any event, the Henderson's violated terms of their rental agreement and were causing problems in the complex.

Mr. Henderson's assertions of being injured on the premises are entirely contrived. He is attempting to defraud the owners of this property. If Mr. Henderson does file a law suit asserting such damages we will file a counter claim against him for fraud and abuse of process. While I have no doubt that a judgment against the Henderson's would be completely valueless we will force Mr. Henderson and his Attorney to defend that case.

After you have had the time to fully investigate your client's assertions, I am sure you will not require our assistance.

Very truly yours,
Mark L. DeLapp
Attorney at Law
April 17, 1990

Re: Darrin K. Henderson

Dear Ms. Jackson:

Fraud: "A deliberate deception for unlawful gain." (American Heritage).

I am in receipt of your certified letter of 4/9/90. I was not surprised to hear from some representation for Mr. Henderson, but I was surprised that an office of your stature and reputation chose to do so.

Mr. Henderson has been making noises and threats ever since I had the police physically evict him. His conduct as a tenant, as verified by several people; their manner of living, as evidenced by my manager, police and county sheriff; and their threats to my manager, would leave one to question his reliability.

There was no collapsing bathroom floor – there was no accident before his eviction. Their 30 day notice was given shortly after occupancy after numerous complaints from adjoining tenants as to the activities causing high traffic rate till early morning hours.

Sarah Brady and Mr. Henderson owe for unpaid rent and court and eviction costs.

Best regards,
Dave DeLapp
May 3, 1990
Dave DeLapp
585 Commercial Street SE
Salem, OR 97302

Dear Dad:

Enclosed is a copy of the letter I received from Kathryn E. Jackson in response to our letter. I am not sure what this means, but I guess maybe she is going to file a suit against DeLapp Real Estate. But then if she doesn't do any more looking into her case than that, she hasn't taken it very seriously. Talk to you later.

Very truly yours,
Mark L. DeLapp
Attorney at Law

April 30, 1990

Mark L. DeLapp
Plaza 125
12606 Southeast Stark
Portland, OR 97223

Re: Darrin Henderson v. DeLapp Real Estate

Dear Mr. DeLapp:

I received your letter of April 24, 1990. No problem, we will do it your way.

With Regards,
Kathryn E. Jackson
May 31, 1991

Mark L. DeLapp
12606 SE Stark
Portland, OR 97233

Re: Darrin Henderson

Dear Mr. DeLapp:

Please be advised that our offices are no longer represent-ing Darrin Henderson for an injury sustained on January 17, 1990. My apologies for any inconvenience this withdrawal may cause your offices.

Best regards,
Kathryn L. Jackson

PADDING THE PROCEDURE
Making my Prothesis

NovaCare O&P West Inc.
1627 N.E. Broadway
Portland, OR 97232
503-287-0459

April 14, 1996

Dear David DeLapp:

We hope you are satisfied with your service we recently provided. To help us serve you better, would you please take a minute and answer the questions below? When completed, simply mail the letter back to us in the envelop provided.

We thank you for your time and hope to continue to serve you in the future.

Thomas Clough
Branch Manager

Dear NovaCare:

I am always disturbed about medical support organizations running up their fees by redundant services that you think no one understands. You underestimate the average person's perceptions and intelligence. I took a good model of my stump that I needed the prosthesis for to your company for another device. Three visits and many hours of time were used to make another to look just like the one I had taken you. We all know your company was running up the bill to be paid by Medicare and my HMO. When I did get the new prosthesis it was made of very inflexible material, hard to get one and off; otherwise, it works alright. Upon requesting a second device, your company said the mold was broken and the second one would have to involve the whole process being done over. If that mold had been preserved, another device could have been made for 20% of the cost of the first one, which you had billed for $3,800.

You asked for my comments.

THE DREAM CAN HAPPEN

Cabin built in 1990 and sold in 2005

Just as an example of how things can change when you lose control is when I was drafted for the Korean War. I left a 112-acre farm with a Grade A dairy, remodeled 3-bedroom home with fireplace, beautiful white painted barn silos, and a mother and dad and older brother, only to return after two years to find they had sold the dairy, bought—without my input—a 160-acre, foothills tree farm in Colton. It had a nice big empty barn and a log house. Yes, an actual 4-bedroom chinked log house—and I thought being drafted was the worst thing that could happen.

Well, that Colton episode is a totally different story and the memory or the vision of that quaint real log house stuck with me for life. So it is with no surprise that 50 years later, in 1990, I bought this beautiful tree covered 2.6 acre piece of solitude and beauty in Mill City. The vision of a secluded log cabin on the bank of the most beautiful river on the USA with nothing but the noise of rushing water revived that old memory.

If ever there was a piece of God-created property that sold itself, this was it. Big tall fir trees, an old weekend cabin that the roof had given up many years ago to moss and rot, and evidence of past family outings on weekends and holidays past, with outgrown lives of exuberant youth and age. I felt the immense solitude and quiet immediately, as has everyone else who has been here. I first thought, why not live here? But the isolated remoteness gave way to the hideaway retreat. No phone, no TV, just me and the river and an occasional elk wandering by my log cabin site. Purchase price: $28,000—

less my half of the commission—leaving $26,000 net. This was never intended to be a short time project.

First of all, some clearing had to be done, so when logging took place down the river I contracted the company to take three loads out, with $12,000 to me, and the provision that, when through, they push the old relic cabin into a ravine against the hill with their CAT and cover it up.

Now I had a spot with some sunlight for grass, no brush, looking like a park—what an enjoyment just to go up and behold, which I did for several years, while I built our home in Lyons on the river in 1996. The old rule in the real estate business is: never fall in love with your property. But, as love so often happens, sometimes you can't help yourself, and so it was with me and that 2.6 acres of secluded river front. In 2003 I'm 75 years old, in love with my own little park when a logger in Elmira advertised poles for sale. When I asked if they would make a log cabin, he got excited. "I was hoping someone would buy them for that very purpose." I did. Sized, peeled, dried, beautiful and cut to length 34 and 22 feet to make my 24×30 cabin. A local band saw operator sided each log to make a tight-fitting, 9-inch-log home.

Everything going great, my dream coming true, except for one small factor: the government. It was zoned EFU (Exclusive Farm Use) under an Oregon law passed in 1995, not allowing any building on EFU property that didn't produce $90,000 per year and my land was growing three Elk. I owned a farm in the valley and was told I didn't need a permit for an Auxiliary Farm Building, so I proceeded to pour a cement slab as the floor to set my auxiliary on. And when it was done, I found a note at the site on a stump, "You need a permit. See Linn County." Signed, "Bob." What "Bob" was doing down at the end of the road through a locked gate I'll never know, but when I went to the county, Bob said, "You need a permit," to which I replied, "You're talking to the wrong man. Your partner in the back room said I didn't, and notes left on stumps are for bootleg whiskey, not for real estate. I will pay your ransom and bring you a plan for a permit."

I finally got it approved for $1,200—a commercial, non-resident building, with a kitchen, bath, 2-bedroom loft, on 2.6 acres on the Santiam River, that looked a hell of a lot like a log cabin. After much work and worry, I finished the project, put in electricity, drilled a well, got my septic permits and sold it to a lumber yard owner who finished it in the prettiest *Sunset* magazine example of the perfect weekend hideaway. He now hides away and I spend his $1,000 per month for my memories. And the memory is rewarded beyond my wildest imagination.

ABE LINCOLN WOULD HAVE BEEN PROUD

WITH YEARS OF TEARS

Our Retirement project. My only way to pay partner's IRS debt. Beginning of the End of partnership.

KENNEDY MOBILE HOME PARK FOR SALE
2009 Kennedy Circle
Keizer, Oregon
(Off Verda Lane on Keizer Road)
85 Space Park Completed in October 1982
This offering made March 1986
For the sale price: $950,000
by
DeLapp Real Estate
858 Commercial Street SE
Salem, OR 97302
for
DeLapp Real Estate in partnership with
Kostenborder Contracting
DBA Delko Development
This confidential form is for the use of the person to whom it is presented and is not for public use. All information is from sources deemed reliable, but is not guaranteed by the agent. Package is subject to price change, corrections, errors, omission, prior sale or withdrawal.

The irony: We built this—worked and worried to get spaces filled. I was a mobile home dealer four years and this was to be our retirement, only to have to sell to pay his IRS debt of $142,000. I added 15 more spaces to the 85. Today in 2015, it grosses $45,000 per month and is worth 4 million dollars.

6

PASSING THE FINISH LINE

MAIN STREET PURCHASE

I bought my lot in Lyons in 1995. Built my house the next year and moved to Lyons in 1996. For 100 years the little town of Lyons had been a logging community with several mills surrounding it and was quite prosperous. Then some brilliant conservationist said that the spotted owl used those trees to nest in and they should be protected. Our government bureaucrats in Washington DC, not knowing where Oregon was, let alone Lyons, agreed with this philosophy and shut down the national forests for logging. This caused the shutdown of many mills, put loggers out of work, left property vacant and caused unbelievable devastation.

When I moved here, I noticed on Main Street a concrete block building on a nice, big lot vacant with a "For Sale" sign on. I couldn't help but conjecture how the building could be used, so passed it by for a couple years. When I became friends with Thurmond Smith the real estate broker, I asked about the building. He said, "Dave you should own that building and rent the house out that goes with it. When I asked what house, he said, "Well, the big two-story house next door and the store building are all priced at $120,000."

It was owned by a woman who is a native of this town and she had let them sit vacant to make them easier to show and sell. I made an offer of $100,000 cash. Her counteroffer was she would take $100,000 but she would not take cash. She said, "I want 39% down and the balance at 10% interest for 10 years with the provision that it can't be sold for five years." I agreed. She had the advice of a lawyer in Stayton and Smith who works for her, and I made it known that I was a real estate broker. We wrote the deal with 39% down balance on a trust deed at $800 a month with the stipulation that in the event

I paid off the balance before five years I would pay a penalty of 5% on the unpaid balance. This was accepted and the deal closed with her attorney drawing the final papers.

I started cleaning up the property, remodeled the house, cleaned up the store building, rented it and made her payments every month. I had reasoned from the very beginning that no mention was ever made that I couldn't escalate a payment monthly, so after the first year I added $10,000 a month to my payment till I reduced the balance to $6,500 which I paid off with the 5% penalty. Her advisors frowned at this but I was totally legal in that and she got her 10% for two years. It's my reason for having that stipulation and I made it very clear that I couldn't buy anything that would restrict me selling it.

I have owned the property 18 years eventually dividing the property into two parcels, creating two tax lots and thereby being able to sell the house on a contract and retaining the store building leased on two-year lease terms. I was able to add five storage units to the commercial building property, which has been easily rented with me keeping one for my own personal use.

I guess I should thank the spotted owl for my gain. I have since built and sold 3 more properties, giving work to local help and business to the hardware store.

Fishing Town of Lyons

I moved to Lyons in 1996. Now living on the beautiful Santiam River. Believe me this is a logging and fishing town. Birthday presents are either Homelite or Pflueger. Sunday school kids think the first four books of the New Testament are Matthew, Mark, Luhr and Jensen. First grade at school includes fly tying and choker setting. The formal dance at high school means no calk boots. Spring break is called spring run with catch and release. Success is a 4-wheel drive F250 and a Willy Drifter.

If Bin Laden really wants trouble, just let him mess with the Mehama-Lyons Bridge where the local fishermen test the water.

PROPERTY OWNERSHIP
A Point of View

This past week I initiated an action that was 180 degrees opposite to my ingrained belief. While doing so I didn't feel good and confused as to my projected goal and therefore it was only partially effective. The impetus for the action was the cutting of timber along the main North Fork of the Santiam River. This cutting took place initially upstream from my residence, across the river, which is my partial view area. The Santiam River is one of the most scenic and pristine rivers of the world. A multitude of people float the 15 mile stretch from Mill City to Stayton just to experience the beauty of the setting. When the timber company proposed to fall timber within 100 feet of the river and completely denude the hills above by clear cutting, my neighbors and I, understandably, became unglued. I made calls to EPA, newspapers, City of Salem (their water supply comes from the Santiam) and I called the Forestry Service. These were actions diametrically opposed to what I believed. But this time, it was my bull being gored. I have always been a property rights advocate.

I have always believed the owner's rights, within the law, come first. If a timber owner, whether he owns one acre or a million, should have a right to harvest his crop when and where he wants. The spotted owl obfuscation (also known as BS) and other impediments were just an interference with that ownership right. I also agree that along with the right to own nature's gifts, comes the right to respect and replenish that resource with good logging practices and replanting that continues the cycle. So here I am. Watching an owner cutting timber he owns, abiding by all the laws and regulations, and destroying a beauty and environment that will be years in recapturing.

Along with my belief in the rights of ownership is the belief that if the public wants the benefits of beauty, serenity and nature preservation, they must pay for it. They should buy it and they should become the owners to reap the harvests of a different nature. Everyone knows in their heart that it is not right to ask private owners to furnish public benefits at their own expense. The purpose of government is not to restrict the benefits of ownership but to promote it, and at the same time, furnish to each of us some protection against overzealousness and perhaps in some cases, greed, that destroys and uses up a natural resource that we can all experience and enjoy. We have public parks, national and state forests: preservation covenants that we own and are enjoyed by all, yet in the process, some situations that need some thinking about. Years ago private companies bought timberland wherever and whenever possible with never the thought of effective water resources for public domain and future use. Now, 100 years later, their concepts and public perception are changing.

How do we reconcile that dichotomy? The timber companies are trying to stay alive, and protect their rights, and some of the public is using illegal means and political pressure to circumvent those rights. Having sold real estate for 45 years has made a believer of me that for every seller there's a buyer and that sometimes two owners have each other's property. The public owns 50% of all the land in the state, some of which they don't know how to use. This is timberland. Timber companies own many parcels better suited to public use than to grow trees (i.e. the Santiam River banks).

Instead of imposing stricter regulations on those who own the scenic property and continued harassments every time they want to fall a tree, I have an alternate solution whereby everyone attains their goal. My example being, I propose to identify these parcels and make an exchange. The public owns the beauty and the company owns the growing timber. This concept isn't new and has been done successfully elsewhere, especially in the Redwoods of Northern California. I know as a tax-paying part of the public I would make someone a good deal if I could exchange a piece of ground I have never seen and couldn't get to for a beautiful and preserved river canyon that can provide peace and quiet for me and generations to come.

It only makes sense that if we want to save it, we better own it. I don't think it needs to be pointed out the advantages to both parties, especially the tax implications for the timber owner. This can and should be done, very simply. Your scenic property for my tree growing property. The first exchange can be precedent-setting for all over the state. Before you log another scenic acre, let me identify a like value (or even a little more) of government owned land that would benefit you. You will have your logs and trees growing and my public co-ownership will have a scenic river undefiled and our water source unmolested. I believe this idea can be sold to the government bureaucrats looking to make both sides of these conservation problems happy. I have exchanged property in the private sector to the mutual benefit of both parties for 45 years; the public interest need not be compromised.

COMMON SENSE AND FAIR DEALING
STARTING IN 1963
Reflecting on how it all started

After three years in the real estate business I knew that this was where I was going to be and when I went on my own as a real estate broker, I knew I was in it for the long haul. So I did a lot of research and used the knowledge that I had gained in the industry over the years, trying to start in with something that people would recognize as me being an individual. During my research, I ran on to this little saying by Ralph Waldo Emerson, "Nothing astonishes men so much as common sense and plain dealing." I read that and said, that's who I am and that's what I want to be recognized for, so I put it on all my correspondence, my cards and so forth, for two purposes.

The first purpose was to create the right feeling between me and a client and a second reason was so that I wouldn't forget the basic feeling of being in the business. I have found out in the last 50 years this was probably the best idea I ever had. More people remembered that more than anything else I've done or said. It also created immediately the feeling that I was working for them. It was an unusual declaration, because at that time, a real estate salesman was just one slight notch above the used car sales. There were a lot of men in the business and, at that time, there were very few women. There were the fast buck artists—the guy who would say anything to make a deal. The retired preacher, and next, the used car salesman. In my previous three years I had recognized those characters and that was my guide to how to conduct myself. There was no one more surprised than I to find out that this model was such an unusual declaration that it was really accepted by people immediately. I never, ever forsook that trust.

The concepts of the real estate business are a wide world and I found that my niche and my interests were in developing—taking a piece of ground and doing something with it. So, it was a very short time to where I was talking to Cecil; he had 30 acres on Brown Road and I really forget how I met him, but he took to me immediately. "Dave, why don't you do something with that." I did; there should be a mobile-home park developed on the site. There hadn't been one developed for several years. I had no money, but I had enough to have plans drawn for a 30-acre mobile home park, which really was about 200 lots— a big project for Dave DeLapp.

It was then that I got my experience with politics, presenting this plan to the planning commission. I was denied with no good reason, except that on the planning commission board was Larry Epping, a developer out on the northeast side of Salem, who wanted to put in a subdivision very close to this and was thinking that the mobile home park wouldn't enhance his development. When I recognized this, I went to Ken Sherman and said that it was politics; he had a very definite conflict of interest.

Ken agreed with me. "Before you appeal this, go, get the three Marion County commissioners and show what you wanted to do, so that when you appeal it, they'll be familiar with the land." The next morning, I picked all three up, showed them that the area explained here was a development-ready location, water and sewer were there, there was no high-priced land around, it was ideal for the developabment of my mobile home park. They agreed but they didn't have guts enough to override the planning commission. The consensus was that it should be a mobile home subdivision, which I was in no position to handle.

I had the option which I presented to a developer out of Portland who came down and got the permit to put in a mobile home subdivision, which had problems I was glad I had avoided. Today it is a division of home owners.

My next venture was an 18-lot subdivision, already divided, with no houses in West Salem. I built 16 houses on the first single lots, but needed a zone change to put four houses on the end double lot, so I applied to the City of Salem for a multiple zone. The problem was, when I showed up at the planning commissioners meeting, there was the gallery full of people from the government low-cost housing development across the same street with a signed petition of 236 signatures, opposing granting my zone change for my rentals. They were all renters, but it was denied. I knew it just wasn't right; first of all the people were renters, but they objected to me putting in rentals.

At that time my representative to the Salem City Council from West Salem was a woman who, when I went to her said, "Dave, that wasn't right, they had no right to object." She went to bat for me to the City Council. They said "That zone will allow you to put any size building you want; will you agree to do four houses, just like what you're saying?" I said, "Absolutely, just four little houses just like I built on the other 16 lots," and built them. (I found out later the manager of the government project had circulated the petition.)

My next project was a five-acre parcel on Sunnyview Avenue, one block off Lancaster, belonging to a retired state worker, who I had gotten acquainted with. There, again, my reputation as being a plain dealer with common sense held up, and he and his wife had 100% confidence in me. I had plans drawn for a small subdivsion, like I had done before, and was ready to present, when two partners from Portland through Doug Nelson, a estate broker, said, "That's a perfect place to put apartments," which was right, so they bought my interests subject to getting a zone change for an apartment complex. This was one of those proposals that, when presented to the planning commission, everyone shows up, including people not affected. The main objection was the traffic that this was going to create. I appealed that decision to the Salem City Council, a special meeting was set up for the hearing, and we were all there. These buyers had hired a specialist from Portland to come down to present their case for a zone change.

The night of the hearing I'm there, Doug Nelson was there,the buyers were there,all the audience was there the whole city council and it was being televised and the big high powered zone change specialist wasn't here. The mayor called ours case to be heard. Someone had to make the presentation I did. I made my apologies to which one of the counselors said he probably got caught in heavy traffic which was the contention of the whole hearing. I had the burden of them reversing the planning commission selling them on our plan for no traffic congestion and the need for more apartments and that they would be an a upgrade to the area. I did it, we got their okay, and the sale was finalized with me gaining a commission, my clients getting all their money and moving to Nevada. Today there is a very nice 150-unit apartment complex there within walking distance of the Lancaster commercial businesses.

My motto of plain dealing and common sense was recognized and it prevailed.

7

LIFE AND LIVING

ANNIVERSARY ACCOLADES

October 6, 2000

Dear Dave,

This is an attempt to let you know that I do love you and some of the reasons why. I admire you in so many ways, your ability to deal with difficult people. The ones who try to get away with anything. Your ability to accept your lack of fingers and go on with your life. Your ability to make good business judgments. Your sense of humor, your pragmatism. Your ability to persevere in difficult circumstances.

Your ability to be tender with pets and babies. The way you can continue to relate to people you have no admiration for and have them admire and respect you in spite of it. Im not always receptive to some of your creative ideas, but I admire the fact that you have them. Your ingenuity never ceases to amaze me. And you are able to complete a job. You can say, "there's, that's done, I'm not going to do any more to that," and walk away satisfied, and not have any doubts about whether someone else would do it differently or better. I like the way you express yourself in writing and storytelling. I find you an amusing and interesting man.

Most of all I appreciate the way you have always kept me informed about what you are doing and thinking, in spite of the fact I have trouble remembering what name goes with which deal, and that numbers do not stay with me. Especially when those two things are important and are what make you so effective in your business. When I thought that I was losing that, it frightened me terribly. I didn't know why at the time, but I think I know now. I would share with you if you would like to know.

Hun

Acknowledgement to Pat's cousins whom I like

Dear Sally and Dick,

Pat knows how much I like you, so she shared your letter with me. I'm sure she explained our situation, and I deduced from your letter you have a pretty clear comprehension of our present lives. To say you were surprised, how do you think I felt when she came home from Salem one day last summer and said, "I've been over to Capital Manor looking at a place to move to." For some unfathomable reason I thought after 38 years our marriage was going to last, and found our marriage is fine, it's me she can't live with. Can you imagine that, me, Mr. Perfect? She was "sad and lonely."

This is not a letter of denial or blame. I have had a family member with an experience of depression so didn't take her feelings lightly, and knew her intentions were real. I have a hard time wrapping my head around the concept of living in a comfortable home, on the banks of a beautiful river, a good income (no debt), in exchange for a 20×20 apartment, one small bedroom, in an environment of 80 year old people with walkers and wheelchairs talking about their health (and lack of it), just to have someone say "you look nice this morning." Pat has been there a month now and seems to be getting settled in, and by God if that makes her happy, who am I to judge? I'm just not ready yet. In fact, if there is anything depressing, it's being surrounded by old people waiting to die. The best thing the place has going for it is the young help in the dining room who serve meals (they seem surprised when I B.S. with them). The food is good, the place is clean, they have all the conveniences of a retirement home and maybe I'm closer to there than I like to think, but not yet. In fact, I play pinochle at the senior center here once a week for three hours; enjoyable, but that's enough. I can stay interested in other things, in fact I just bought another house in Lyons. It was so cheap I couldn't pass it up. I have a contractor who is willing to work cheap and do the whole remodel. I do an excellent job overseeing.

I miss living with Pat. I suggested many alternatives to her moving out even to the extent of building a duplex and always having a housekeeper next door, but nothing fit. She thinks coming over will be sufficient but I know that will soon get old. Then perhaps one of us will change our course. In the meantime—one of the plusses of being married to her was how nice her family is, and even though I see a lot of her mother in her, I liked the old lady, and had fun with your whole clan. So I still barbeque a mean steak and have a bottle of vino for anyone willing to put up with us for an afternoon on the deck by the river. I know it is a little hard for relation and friends to put get-togethers in its proper perspective but we are still a couple, we are not divorced, don't hate each other and I hope will still go places together, we just live apart most of the time (with me paying the bills). I'm still looking forward to that dinner with Mike and Denise at Kings winery.

I still get e-mail. Drop me a note, here at the river lodge.

Dave

P.S. Sally, that knee surgery was no walk in the park was it? You guys have had more leg, ankle and knee trouble in the last few years than most left tackles. When I told my doctor I broke a leg in two places, he said, stay out of those places.

FRIEDA

Her 85th Birthday Party at Willamette Manor

On August 13, 1966 a woman walked into my office looking to rent a house that I had. On August 13, 1975 I married that woman who came with the package of two kids, and a friend Frieda. The two kids weren't a gold mine, but Frieda has been a delight. Both being nurses at the same hospital, they had become close friends with the common problems of being divorced, kids and making a living. Frieda was not entirely a stranger to me because we had gone to high school together in Salem. She played in the band (and I don't know what instrument, probably a banjo for all I know). Being at a school of 1,800 kids, and she two grades behind me—I never knew her, but Frieda Carlson was part of the scene. When I first knew her she had three kids, Pat had two. So their conversations went something like, "Now take my kids, please." They both came through that with my help and very little input.

When Frieda's kids all went on their own, she had the big house to get rid of—which she did—and then bought into this old people's home. But the only thing is, Frieda never got old. She really thought it was a retirement home, and just a nice place to stop off between taking trips. She has seen more of this world than Hillary Clinton. She remembers them all and can recite for hours on hours about her travels and the people she met. In fact, the only time she stops talking is to catch her breath. So the wonder of it all is that here we are. I'm going on 87, she is 85, the wife is 83. She has been a lifesaver to us all. When you think of the word "Godsend" you can think of Frieda. That word says it all.

8

FAMILY

DOING FIFTY

REMEMBRANCE BY ASSOCIATION

Just the words create the beginning of memories and so here is a list of old remembrance words. Logan berries—blackberries—cleaning chicken house—picking nuts—outdoor toilet—the old house kitchen—old lady Renner—Bob the collie—all dressed up going to the fair—waiting for daddy—goat—pigs—lamb—chickens and new straw—oat and vetch hay—Buster the horse—Lila the kicker—riding the horse drawn crop masher—watering the horse—Ma Perkins at 12:15—Pepper Young's family—Amos and Andy—Lum and Abner—gangbusters—set on train—streamlined wagon—house burning down—new two roomed house—hot wood stove—George Hall—picking prunes—eating cherries—the old road to Renner's place—old chicken house with dirt floor—the path to the river, our swimming hole—the island—turkeys—tomatoes—alfalfa—Jerry—turkeys—milking—John Deere corn planter from Hogg's—plowing—mowing—hauling manure—the train tracks and logging trains—Gervais—cows—the original farm—the rock garden—fish pond and wooden bridge—past the chicken house, the picket fence—Bob's rotor rooter—electric fence—my buddy dump—waiting for dad Saturday night with bananas—fried chicken—apple pie—warm kitchen—canning peaches—room in the basement—putting in wood-stacking—warm furnace registers—sleeping with Bub—Christmas morning—jumping on the bed—Sunday school and Mrs. Deiters—the view from the end of the line. Lots more laughing than crying.

MOM

Mom was 80 in 1973 and moved into her new house on Clarmar, which I had built for her. To all of her brothers' and sisters' relief and blessing, Sister Sammy moved from Ephrata, Washington, moved in with our mother, and took care of her. Most importantly, she did this not as a duty but as something she wanted to do—"I get as much out of living with mom as she does."

Mom was lucky, among all of her seven kids there wasn't one that she couldn't be proud of, and there was not one grandchild that she ever had to apologize for. She might point out the flaws in everyone else's kids and even criticize her own, but she really knew these were temporary and the bad would pass and leave the good. Neat and orderly? Only when company was coming. The petty chores got done but their importance of when was low on her list. A clean kitchen got no considerations when 15 pigs needed to be kept warm by the kitchen's gas range and fed every hour. A mopped floor wasn't nearly as much fun as having a lamb come right into the house for his bottle and seeing the family laugh their heads off. A clean chicken house with fresh right straw and pretty white chickens pleased her more than a sparkling house. She was a farmer, a gardener, cook, an interior decorator, crocheter, needlepoint rug maker and painter with an eye for beauty, color, quality, character, and honesty.

MY DAD

I 've always thought I should be able and owed an effort to write about my dad. I need to try to characterize him to make a memory with meaning. First statement: We were not close as some depictions of father-son relations have been made. We never ever had that "father-son talk" but there was never any doubt who was who. It's the old saying, "He may not be right, but he's the boss." I was the youngest of seven and now I feel in retrospect he let the older ones guide me, but he made the rules and they were never questioned. That is not necessarily bad and he provided for the family better than many in those days of depression. His morals were good, he neither smoked nor drank, he cussed some, laughed and told stories, liked animals and his wife, our mother.

A man of little personal praise for the kids, but demonstrable pride in things we did. There were three sons, the two oldest in WW2—over which he worried; but when they came home safe he never hugged them nor bragged about them, only showed relief, and thought that was over in his lifetime—then what happened?

Five years later we were in another war and I was drafted. Dad never let on he was bothered. That October afternoon he drove me to the bus depot in Salem to board a Greyhound full of draftees to take us to the induction center and all he said was "Chip, take care of yourself and write us." A bewildered, and up 'til then protected, farm boy got on the bus.

It was then, looking out the window, I saw my father cry for the first time.

9/13/08

My Dear Brother,

Although we are both getting near the end of our time in this life that has been given to us, I can't help feeling a sense of youth in writing this to you. But it's now or never. We are constantly told, "Don't wait too long," and then we do, and then regret our procrastination. Here are some things I should have said long before.

Bub you were always my idol, my mentor, my confidant and although only 6 years older in years, so much more mature that you gave me love and caring, our father never gave me. It was Bub who rode me to school on his bike. It was Bub who taught me to drive a car. It was Bub who looked out for me swimming. It was Bub who took me with him to make a fortune splitting wood one summer and I don't remember questioning his judgement then, or now.

Six years difference in age isn't much now, but when I was 10 or 11, you were 17. A kid and a man. How I looked forward to Friday nights when I might get to watch you play football and have you tell me all about it. And how I cried when sometimes Dad wouldn't take me with him. He never knew how much that hurt. I was one sad kid when you got married, sure I had lost you, but you never let that happen.

I always felt that if Bub says "it," IT was so. You fixed the old GMC 1927 truck and said, "Chip, you can handle this now," and at only 16, I did. Moving us, hauling feed, hauling cows, just because Bub said I could.

The Gervais farm was my growing up time. And it was you who bought that paint pot and compressor and said, "Chip, you can paint this house, garage, barn, dog, cat and tractor." Bub said, "I'll show you how to solder these wires to re-wire the upstairs in the house" This was the time of starting your own family, and you didn't slight them by keeping an eye on me. The love, and respect you have enjoyed from your children and their families shows how much you gave them.

You never tried to interfere with my life, but you were always ready with an idea, suggestion or advice in watching me struggle to make a living on my own. It was Bub who said, "Why don't you go down and talk to Reiman and Lucas about selling real estate? You certainly must have as much smarts as Ed Lucas and he's doing well." I did, and because they 'knew Glen', I started down that road that has never ended. It was when I started back working in Salem that I became aware of the reputation of Glen Delapp. How many times have I said, "Yes, he's my brother," and my status became immediately elevated in their eyes. It was always you who gave me confidence and never once indicated doubt in what I attempted. And how many times have I said to myself, 'Bub wouldn't think that was right.' You have guided my conscious more than I ever thought. We are who we are and what effect anyone has on us, on our character, can never be determined for certain. We can only look back and ask, "Who would I have been without the influence and love of those around us? Bub, my life is fuller, more comfortable, and happier because of you. I can only hope you derived a sense of self-satisfaction in seeing me succeed, you were the major factor.

Chip

Bub died in his sleep 9/2/2008.

The Salutation of the Dawn

Listen to the Exhortation of the Dawn!
Look to this Day, for it is Life -
In its brief course lie all the Verities
And Realities of your Existence
The Glory of Action,
The Splendor of Beauty;
For Yesterday is but a dream,
And Tomorrow is only a vision;
But Today well lived
Makes every Yesterday a Dream of Happiness ,
And every tomorrow a Vision of Hope.
Look well, therefore, to this day!
Such is the Salutation of the Dawn.

—*Author Unknown*
From the Sanscrit

DUMP AND CHIP AND OTHER BLOSSOMS
PHOTO: BEN MAXWELL

CHAPTER EIGHT

LETTER TO JEAN

Dear Dump,

This letter is of no significance whatsoever so don't look for
any. But what a beautiful April 13—if today was Easter I
could get religious—instead I will have to just account some
power to creating it.

The early pink Rhodies are at their prettiest. The bright
reds are opening up and my 5 tulips are standing alone
but trying to look beautiful, and the lawn is mowed and
trimmed. Wonder of wonders when Patrick cleaned the
leaves out of my pond yesterday, what showed up but my big
goldfish, 8 inches long, that we'd thought was long gone to
raccoons. If there ever was a day made to just sit and look at
a beautiful river, it is today, and two old farts are doing more
than just looking. They are anchored right out front in my
hole trying to catch a Steelhead—good for them. It is clear,
the sun is sparkling on the ripples and my old goose is setting across on the island—should be about hatching time.
Pat was home Friday night, too bad she can't enjoy this as
much as I do, but I'm a simple man—it doesn't take much
(they had to close down her dining hall, all the old people
getting sick. They are giving the food away, no activities, no
Sunday brunch). If I were there, (I don't think I'll ever be)
I'd head to Hawaii.

Just thought I would write you a note as a contented man
this morning—sitting here wanting to thank you for my
hand blown glass vase—all part of a sunny scene.

Love, Chip

JULY 9, 2001

Dear Dump,

Because Hallmark hasn't known you very personally for the past seventy five years, I thought I would make this weak (though not as witty or clever) attempt to wish you a happy birthday for a diamond anniversary. Nothing in the book says how big the diamond should be (on a diamond anniversary) but the Hope is about the right size.

Just put 75 years in perspective. Seventy-five years before you were born, the Civil War had not been fought, the Oregon Trail had just been started, gold had just been discovered and Oregon wasn't a state. What a time we've lived. So the 75 years since you were born have been probably the most important time of any similar period of all time. Whether the "progress" has been all good probably won't be known for another 75 years.

I'm sitting here on my deck looking at two young swallows coming to the hole in their safe little house in our redwood tree and looking out. They've been hatched and fed and now it's time to fly—my God how big and vast that world must look to them. Hell, they don't even know if they can fly until they get out on that perch and jump! They don't know how big that world really is till they start the journey of life. I don't know if daddy Swallow has told them what to expect, but it probably doesn't make any difference; all he can really do is breed into them the ability to fly, the rest is up to them, and boy do they have some surprises in store for them.

So, from the hottest day in '26 when you were born, to the prettiest day of '01, you've flown your course. Of those

27,394 days, some were unpleasant, most were good, some were great but not on one of them were you ever not Jean (Dump). She flew with her own wings and still flying to new heights. No pretense—no put on—no flash—no fake. My sister of substance, wit, smarts and level head. Not always right, but always Dumpling.

This little brother can only say how glad I am to have been able to fly with you some of the times.

Thank God you have never gotten old.

Love! Chip

WE ALL GOT OLDER

July 10, 2003

Jean's birthday

Little "Dumpling" has another one (she was little Dumpling 77 years ago and is a little Dumpy today). Even though she started out as Dumpling, is it only remarkable that every birthday was an accounting of every year and now it's like "Oh, I'm somewhere between 75 and 80." The old half-empty/full water glass cliche now applies to anniversaries. Is it another year of happy, fruitful, thanks-for-living life or, another year closer to the end? Maybe we can't celebrate in as an exuberant manner as when younger, but we can make up for it in happy reflections and warm anticipation of another day, week or year of love. Now the contentment comes from within. It's been a day to celebrate for 77 years—not really significant, only a reminder to enjoy.

Chip

SOME GOOD THINGS MUST END

I sold mom's house on Nebraska for $95 which added to her social security and made her very comfortable. When she died at the age of 89, rather than divide the $95.00 payment from the house each month all ways, I created a family dinner fund at the bank, for which we each—seven and spouses— had holiday dinners after Christmas, and birthday dinners as we reached 70 and 80. These dinners were at the nicest place in town, usually the Prime Rib being the favorite, with the private executive room. We went through 70 just fine with the $70 birthday tree and the oldest three did their 80's, but come Jean's 80th, the oldest had passed on, and the next two were in no shape to travel. Jean's husband was nearly 90 and in bad shape, so Jean said, "Chip, I know we've always celebrated being 80, but let's forget mine, it's just too much stress." So, this following is my letter.

For Jean, born on the 10th of July, 1926
(Dump is a family nickname)

Dear Jean,

Well, you didn't want a big ta-doo for your fore score, (and here I thought I had an unbroken precedent), so the next best thing is an unsolicited testimonial and personal scribbling, of a sibling, on such an occasion. After recognizing all of the silly Hallmarks and candle blowing, it all comes down to eighty years is pretty damned good and covers a lot of ground and is a time to reflect. At first my reflection is—all my brothers and sisters have done it so I've got a pretty good shot too. My second is that of all the DNA's passed down, I think you've got more of Mom's. Even though you didn't have 8 kids, or crochet a table cloth or raised chickens, those other spirited things come through that are Dump and/or Mom and that's not only good but continues to be amazing to me. Last thought is the old bromide of, "What an eighty you've seen." From horse and plow to millions of people flying through the air watching television, this only leaves that same old question, with maybe a different meaning, "What's this old world coming to?"

Write me when I'm eighty (maybe sooner)? Picnic is August 13, hope all is well for you two to make it. Fish is good for you, a laugh or two even better.

Love, Chip

Note: That Sunday afternoon on her birthday, I picked up my brother and we went to their place with a Chinese dinner from Kwans in Salem where they love to go to, and we had a little dinner at her place anyway. Second note: I found a little wooden carving that said, "I'm smiling because you're my sister, I'm laughing because you can't do anything about it." She says she has it hanging above her range.

ETHEL THE OLDEST SISTER

When I'm at a funeral and someone gets up to say a few words I always think, "Well, what is this guy going to say and will it be of any interest or just rambling?" Well, I'll tell you right off, this is just rambling, but shouldn't one of us ramble a little? In Ethel's obituary there was the designation of homemaker. She was the epitome of homemakers. She did it with class; she elevated dusting to an art. Dinner at Ethel's was always a dining experience. Her home was always warm—warm with kitchen smells, warm with decorations, and warm with her spirit. You couldn't be sad or down very long with Ethel.

Her marriage to Sam started in the depression years. There must have been some tough times but the bright lights always shown with Ethel. Ethel and Sam didn't have the same ideas about traveling. He would go fishing and hunting, but long auto trips north and south were not his thing. Ethel liked going and eating out. She could have been talked into living in Palm Springs. She went there several times to see and to stay with Francie Feller, her longtime friend. The shopping and eating places were her idea of living. She could remember and tell about every good place to eat between here and Palm Springs, and what the specialty of the house was. She really hated it when Francie moved back to Salem and she no longer had an excuse to go south.

I remember her relating how at 17 she wasn't the happiest girl in the world when I was born. After all it was a new baby to look after every two years for 17 years. No wonder she held off for 18 years to have her one and only. Sam was a good father and Ethel had mothering down pat. Tim never wore a dirty shirt or un-pressed pants in his life, but he was not spoiled nor did he ever want. The pride of mother and father kept him on the straight and narrow she was justly proud. His 51 years of life was a time of joy. His wives had a lot to live up to in order to measure up to Ethel. I have often wondered how I would have turned out if Ethel had not left home when I was five. She changed Sam from a backwards unsocial country boy who hid in our closet during an open house of our new home and changed him to a very successful salesman who could meet anyone of any social standing. He always wanted to look good in her eyes and be successful for her and that was Ethel's influence; we all did. When Ethel bragged about you, you had arrived, you were making it in this world.

A LIFE OF LOVE

a Georgina Beth advocacy of living

It's only because of an anniversary of a long ago birth date that we stop and reflect on who you are and what you did and why. You may have made it look easy but it has been your natural way to smooth the rough spots and flatten the bumps. Encouraged the discouraged, strengthened the weak, and sympathized and not criticized. Pat will always fondly remember you as the family member who invited us to dinner and plays in Eugene at the Hult Center. I will always keep the personal note you wrote on my 50th birthday. Beth, you had more influence on me than you'll ever know. You without a doubt had more aspirations for a future when you were young than any of the rest of us. You were the only one to go to college, and to this day I have no idea how you did it. Your higher level thinking of achievements was not lost on me entirely, all of which is exemplified by your marriage, your family, your friends, and your lifestyle. You have made class a bright light of character.

Love, Chip

ON BIRTHDAYS

*On the occasion of Georgina Beth (DeLapp) Berge's 80th
birthday, celebrated at the traditional family dinner party,
with her three sisters, Ethel, Sammy, and Jean, and three
brothers, Glenn, Perry, and David, the following essay was
presented.*

The person who decided we should measure our age by years
of the anniversary of our birth was absolutely 100 percent
wrong. He knew nothing about aging and less about living.
We all know getting old is a thought process and that process
starts at different times of each person's life. Being slower,
being grayer, being fatter may be related to years but not necessarily to being old. George Burns said at 96, "I'm getting
older, but I'm not getting old." So what is getting old? It's
when we let the bad thoughts outnumber the good thoughts.
Good times, lots of laughter and doing things that make us
feel good make us young. Anger, resentment, jealousy and
the like make us old. Therefore, each day we live either adds
or subtracts from our real age. So today how old are you
really? I think your laughs and goodness have so outnumbered negatives that your youth can be celebrated rather than
getting old. So Beth, have a Happy Life Day.

Written and read by Dave, March 9, 1996.
Beth's birth date was February 22, 1916.

Eulogy at Howard's Funeral

At his church in Eugene
He was 94

I'm Chip. Howard's brother in law for 69 years. Beth was
one of my four older sisters who was independent in a nice
way. She knew where she was going and how to get there.
So when she met this tall handsome 6'2" Swede officer,
he never had a chance. And, Howard could wear a uni-
form like no one else I ever knew. He was one good looking soldier and he hadn't just fallen off the turnip truck
either. Beth was a smart, good looking woman with a car
and access to rationed gas, and he was a warrant officer of
the 96th division, the business officer, stationed at Camp
Adair. We often said it was a good thing that he knew how
to handle money, because Beth always had ideas on how to
spend it.

We had a little farm with a tractor which qualified us for
rationed gas. Well, you know that gas burned in a car just as
well as in a tractor. So who put the gas from the barrel into
the 1936 Plymouth? Young, 15 year old Chip. So Howard
and his lifelong friend Berdette had transportation from
Camp Adair to see Beth and her lifelong friend Betty Rae.
Chip became an accomplice and a buddy, and later a relation
for life. No one ever questioned how such a small little farm
used so much gasoline. I mention my nickname because
only family calls me that (I didn't know my name was David
until I started school), and Howard, in his affable style,
used it in the beginning like an old family member. I believe
he probably never expressed anger in his life. You knew
Howard arrived at a dinner or picnic when we heard that
deep gutted laugh that was so infectious, the world could

use more of that. Finally, about his family. How lucky could three girls be to have as respected a father in business and friendship as Howard Berge. He was the epitome of character, honesty, humor and genuine kindness. He lived and died in peace. Our lives are richer because Howard was part of it. It's easily understood by our family why the congregation of this church would choose to honor he and Beth with your beautiful stained glass window.

FEARLESS BUB

On his eightieth birthday

In 80 years, how many things has Bub built or fixed? I wasn't there the first few years, but it wouldn't surprise me if he made his own diaper drying rack. Ever since I can remember, everything built had Bub's stamp on it.

He graduated pretty quickly from rope-steered carts to our 4-bedroom house. He was 14 or 15 when we started building the house, after the fire took the old one. And of course, Dad didn't make it easy, he had to have a basement. Now I don't know how big that basement actually was, but I do know that an excavation 30×30×6 ft. is 200 cubic yards all done by manpower and horse power and and lots of Bub power. No wonder nothing ever fazed Bub later on. The house got built, but at the same time, so did a dandy chicken feed bin with 2 compartments and a tight fitting lid. Then there was the chicken brooder house, built in a hexagon shape so that it had no right angled corners for chicks to pile up in and get smothered. Then there were the picket fences, a decorative bridge and really neat garden wheel barrow with removable sides, and a diving board that was improved and replaced every year, down by our swimming hole.

Then how about the near genius electric brooder with the thermostat regulated heating coils under a wire meshed floor that kept chicks warm from underneath. That item was made up in component parts that disassembled for cleanup.

The building list goes on for another 65 years, including remodeling every house Mom and Dad bought, and a true log house on the Colton frontier. When we needed a building, it was, "Bub, can you build us a . . . ?" And fearless Glen had no hesitation. At the same time as all these endeavors were happening, Bub was also repairing the farm machinery when it broke down. He is NOT one dimensional.

But these are later stories that we siblings have all experienced. When necessarily dictated by invention, Bub did and does today, have the answers.

Chip

MOTHER'S SISTER

On Aunt Pauline's death

Dear Verda Lou,

Thank God there are still good people like yourself left in this world. Your thinking of others and compassion for them is surely appreciated and we distant cousins do thank you for caring and calling. I know why you were mom's favorite niece.

It's always a sad day when a relation dies. We know your closer relationship makes it even more difficult and we do thank you for making her last years comfortable.We know that you have spent many dollars and hours in taking care of Aunt Pauline. We all agreed that mom would want us, as a way of remembering her, to express that thanks to you, who did so much for her. We know that you do good because that in itself is a reward, but Verda Lou we give this small gift as our thanks and love.

To Mark on his Birthday

January 24, 2000

On January 24, 1958 I felt I got short-changed. The first baby, a little over 2 years before cost at $400 or $50.79 per pound, but on 1-24-58 I got less baby for the same $400 which figured $60.00 per pound. Not only did I start out behind but I've had to put more feed in him to grow him out. Even thought for a while he might be a runt for life. But the genes were there so he fattened out alright. The number 3 came bigger but the price had gone up so I never did recoup my loss.

Happy B-Day.
Dad

(P.S. I didn't have anything to do with all this but in my opinion he got a good bargain. Pat)

Jay,

I have been going through relics of my past experiences, in the process of cleaning up the attic and accumulations in my office. In that process a revelation has occurred. I keep finding small seemingly insignificant little mementos of your caring for your dad which when put together comprise a deeper feeling than is evidenced by my other two children. Jay, I feel ashamed in some degree that at the moment I missed the feeling you were trying to show. It was Jay who mounted a pen holder on a beautifully finished myrtle wood block—It was Jay who polished a petrified rock with a pen holder for my desk—a desk of clear plastic with his picture imbedded. A small strip of green laminate with the very plain precise, "I love you." I've kept them all but it has taken 35 years to begin to understand the feeling behind each one. I hope in all these years I haven't given the idea of taking you for granted and have been a dad in my own best way. I get emotional now about all my kids, I know it might have helped to show sooner. I tried to show my love and caring but I could have said it more often. It was there, but that's the dad you got. You got to me the other night when you said, "Where we going fishing this year?" If I'm able I don't want to miss the chance. I told a friend of ours how proud I was of my kids. Her reply was, "Have you told them?" My wife is always reminding me I should. Your little thoughtful homemade items remind me how important I am to you and hope I have shown my love in my own way. I am getting old—but not too late.

Dad

LETTER ABOUT VAN LYNN

Dear Mark:

Think very seriously about using your knowledge to the benefit of a developer who needs someone to change a land use—zone changes. Partner up with him (without fees) but percent of the action—they all hate to fight City Hall and you can do the job no one else wants to do.

I have been very successful in every application when I knew I was right. Changing uses of land can double it's value very easily and there are lots of opportunities for the person who is willing to fight the battle. When you get involved in the first stage, the rest of the program falls into place, i.e. building, developing, leasing, etc., and you are a principle.

I know Mark Lee—he has an Alpha-Romeo complex. The thing that he also has is the ability to earn that status and be respected by everyone while he does it. You're lucky - you've got all the equipment and your luck gets better the harder you work.

You are going through a midlife crisis but it's not as the term usually is defined. The midlife is very evident: Educated, established, family, good income. The crisis is how do you satisfy that unique accomplishment recognition - the Alpha-Romeo complex? You probably never realized how much I gained by developing Van-Lynn subdivision. I did that by myself - my idea, my negotiation, my work, my selling of the houses, and the topping on the cake was being able to give Mom a pretty little home to spend her last years in. God, I've been proud of that. My daughter's name will be on the subdivision record, forever, and I'll always pat myself on the back. From there I progressed to bigger and better, and there's more to accomplish.

It takes balls and just plain doing what you know is right. Pride is based on knowing what other people think of you.

Love,
Dad

LYONS, OREGON

July 4, 2007

Dear Brothers and Sister, and all other Affiliates:

Subject: Annual Family Picnic

You may have noticed at the last couple of picnics the three legged potato sack race has degenerated to who can walk unassisted. That dog isn't just a pet, he's a guide. More fried chicken goes home unmolested, and one fish feeds the multitude. So if the fun is gone, and the ranks have depleted, and raising the flag is harder to salute, and I have decided to not have the Family bust here this year. Every year becomes harder, and sitting around in the shade eating somehow isn't the attraction it used to be.

If any of the youngsters want to keep alive this long honored tradition, God Bless. And if anyone wants to bring an old dead chicken or steer to barb-b-que by the river and eat on our deck, you don't need to wait for an invitation.

Nicholas was an only child of Mark and Marilyn, given anything he wanted and over-protected. A nice kid—reserved but never left to his own decisions.

1ST LETTER

To grandson Nicholas (my last hope for descendant fame):

You can't begin to know the pleasure I got from recieving your report card. I was not surprised by your four "A's" (well, maybe a little on Shakespeare, I THOUGHT YOU WERE PULLING GRANDPA'S LEG ABOUT BEING YOUR FAVORITE SUBJECT) and doubt if the reward factor helped much, but it can't hurt having a little additional motivating factor, so let's expand on that a little. Old Grandpa notices on those subjects you got "A's," there is a possibility that there may be more bullshit skills than actual learning. The two others with the "C's" are math and physics which take a little more diligence and work and thinking. If you have those classes next semester, show me an A in each and I'll up the ante to $200, and still give the $100 in each of the others. As old William S. said, "To be or not to be, that is the question," it's up to you.

Your dad called and said you had been accepted to either Oregon State or Southern Oregon and haven't heard back from U of O yet. Sounds great you made the cut, they will be harder, but we don't want them saying, "Wherefore art thou Nicholas?" B.S. goes aways in this world, but a degree goes a lot further. We are all behind you.

Keep in touch. I'm accompanying this with the note that $400 has been added to your college account, plus it is adding stock value gain every month, so every time the stock market goes up, you get richer.

2ND LETTER

Letter I call his maturing responsibility letter

Dear Nicholas,

READ THIS CAREFULLY

Today you are 18—the age everyone says you are a man, and being a man has automatically placed upon you the responsibilities of your personal behavior and your personal goals and hopefully your personal future.

Up until now, these have been within the pervue of those who have nurtured and love you, who care about you. Their dictates, suggestions, allowances, directions and discipline have been made through love and caring about making Nick the best person he can be taking advantage of this desired effect. From here on out, further advice and directions are only suggestions, i.e. Nick has to make up his own mind. Nick has to choose his own friends, Nick has to decide the character he will portray on which he will be judged by others. Nick has to begin choosing his future course on what he wants to be and where he wants to go. Other people will now influence your character but you are now at the age to decisively determine what character that man shall show for the rest of his life. You have been raised a very lucky boy, cared for by a mother and a father who have devoted their whole being to Nick's comfort, welfare, needs and moral integrity, to make you a person of pride and respect. As your grandfather, I have shared in that feeling. Out of respect for their intense feeling for you, I have restricted my influence to a minimum as any need to interfere was never needed. You have been a great grandchild and as last of the line, you shall always continue to do so. I have been fortunate in having the opportunity to help the others in their education but only when they showed their appreciation by working hard on their grades, making me proud of them. You are getting to that stage in life to seriously consider your next step. If you need help I'm offering my help, but I need communication about what you are doing to prepare—grades—interests—what college or preparation you want. In other words, Nick, do you want help, or even need it? We tried to phone on your birthday with no response but realize it was a busy time for you. But, the world doesn't run on automatic. You have to use your turning signals for us to know where you're going. I would like to help.

NICK'S REPLY TO GRANDPA

September 4, 2013

Dear Grandpa:

I want to tell you I do appreciate you helping me go to college. I did thank you and I meant it, and appreciated that you gave me the money. I used it for room and board which is $2,200.00 a term and I went 3 terms. The majority was used in 2013 again for room and board. I may be quiet but I really do appreciate you helping me! I'm not that great at responding to anyone on the phone.

I am not rude to anyone. I am sorry you feel that I let you down but I did try to find a part-time job which was not easy in a college town, especially without a car. I also have a lot of responsibilities in my house and in college in general. My classes are not easy and also take up a lot of my time.

I interviewed for a job two days after my term ended in June and started work a couple days later. I have worked all summer for a company in Clackamas, actually two companies but mostly at one. My hours are Monday–Friday, 6am–2pm or when the work is done. The Daimler strike has hurt my hours. I made $10 per hour. I drove truck, did inventory, put parts together, helped with shipping and receiving and whatever else I was told. I am working through next Wednesday and have to be back at school on Friday to prepare the house for the year, Rush, etc.

I have grossed to date $2,676 total from both companies. I have deposited every check and not cashed any for expenses. I will get one last check for my last week before I return to school. I haven't done much of anything except work and help dad move some furniture and build a trellis. I guess it is up to you whether you think I deserve help with college or not. I met with my advisor a couple weeks ago. I have a C+ average to date. College is not easy but I really enjoy Corvallis and college. I have not found my niche as far as a degree but my advisor said I have a solid base for many different degrees whether I major or minor in business.

Grandpa, thank you for helping me with college.

Nick Delapp

9

PERSONALITIES

GRANDPA MARTEL

I have determined that the heritage for longevity derives from my mother's side of the family. All seven of her children have lived past 85 years old and four of them lived to 90. I never knew her mother, but I did meet my grandfather once when he came to Oregon with his youngest daughter, my aunt, when he was 84 years old. His name was Oscar Martel. He was a descendent of the French Martels and Charlemagne. When my son went to college he studied about Charlemagne and went overboard to the extent that he gave his only child the middle name of Charlemagne.

Oscar Martel was born and raised in southern Illinois. He lived through four wars and half of the fifth. I saw him for a few days' visit when I was nine years old and he was 84, so I can only make up his wonder of living today. From his obituary, his 94 years were fruitful, proud years; a man of character who neither smoked nor drank, had ten children, raised seven (one son, six daughters), always commented on living from Lincoln to Truman and, as far as that was concerned, he said, "Too bad the wrong man was shot."

I like to think today he could take life in stride. He started young as a poor farmer, accepted his role as someone people admired and wound up owning the bank in Sesser, which he lost in the 30s depression. This was a hard blow, and he always bragged that no one lost a cent in his bank, but it broke him. He rode in horse and buggy and flew in a new airliner. He saw the telegraph invented and watched television. He witnessed the invention of the Smith & Wesson revolver and the atom bomb, so, extremes would not faze him. I'm sure his only comment today would be that this world sure is going to hell.

LEON

H e's just another Leon," is a familiar phrase in our family. This exemplifies the ultimate in character and personality of a cousin who all know as Leon Hammerly. He was my dad's nephew, one of two sons of his oldest sister, and progeny of her first husband (who was the first of three and others who should have been). Being dad's older sister and having Leon when she was young made dad just a few years older than Leon, so the bond was more of a sibling nature, but my parents were always Uncle Bud and Aunt Bertha to Leon.

Leon was a natural salesman which meant he handled the truth pretty recklessly. He had Uncle Bud sold but not Aunt Bertha. It was usually without warning that dad would look out the window and say, "Well, there's Leon," to which mom would reply, "Oh shit, we've got to put up with that blowhard for another three days." But mom never showed it, and he had uncle Bud's homemade ice cream with his saying, "Chip there's a block of ice and some speckled bananas in the back of my car." So we got out the hand cranked White Mountain ice cream freezer, made our ice cream, and Bertha had fried chicken and apple pie.

Leon became the metaphor for anyone who never stopped talking, might stretch the truth, but was never offensive. Leon led a life that someone should record and make note of. If ever there was a rags to riches, the poor boy makes a good story. Leon lived it. He and his brother rode the rails from Kansas City out to Salem, and by that it means underneath freight cars to rails up off the track that a man can lie in. He and his brother came to Oregon that way.

When he got here he had taken up radio, and—actually— he was a genius. In 1930, he sat in our living room and made a radio. He went on to selling appliances with the biggest appliances store in Salem, owned by a fellow named Herb Stiff, who knew dad well. He said, "Bud, Leon is the best salesman I have in the building." From there, he got wind of an appliance store in Medford, Oregon, owned by a woman who was looking for someone to operate it with her financial backing. This was the promised land for Leon Hammerly. He went down there, talked his way into it, and had an appliance store that he ran for two or three years selling Philco radios and appliances. Our first refrigerator was a Philco which he got for Uncle Bud at cost.

But just like people without any experience, when Leon got a few bucks he blew it, and eventually, in 1940, he got to writing bad checks and had to leave Medford, his mother said, because the FBI was after him. He went back to Kansas City, but they were still after him, so his only solution was to go to Alaska, out of the United States. He talked himself into being a maintenance man for the Civil Aeronautics Administration (CAA); they flew him all over the territory of Alaska setting up radio beams for landing planes on airports during the war. He would come out to see us and Marie in Seattle once a year, then go back to Anchorage and eventually got married again.

When the war was over, he had worked himself up to being an executive with CAA and eventually became the administrator for maintenance for all Alaska. In 1954, dad and mom drove the Alcan Highway to Alaska to see Leon, and when dad walked into the CAA office, the receptionist said, "Oh! Uncle Bud with the banana ice cream. It's known all over Alaska." It was then he learned that Leon had become the administrator for the whole region and had to have special dispensation from Washington, D.C. to allow him to accept a position without a college education—the only time it had ever been done, before or after.

His knowledge in the field was so good that, during the war, he was independent enough to say, "If you don't like the way I do it, find someone else." He gave Uncle Bud and Aunt Bertha the royal treatment, showing them glaciers, going fishing, and even inventing a maintenance trip, flying to Point Barrow, the top of the world. Of course, he didn't stop drinking—or fishing—and he had to come out once a year to the racetracks, lose his money, and go back up to do his job.

So the description of someone being "another Leon" has many facets and one thing that stood out in our minds was that Leon was a brilliant man. After he died, his widow wrote a letter saying that Leon had left it in his will that when she sold their property, if there was anything left in the estate, that she would give some to Babe and Chip, which she did. He died soon after retiring at 57 and chose to be buried in Salem, next to Uncle Bud and Aunt Bertha.

LUCILLE

O ne of my best friends in my life was a woman to whom I was not married. It is not only possible, but very normal, for two people of the opposite sex to be socially compatible with the total exclusion of sexual interaction. I was raised in a large family with paternal dominance in the depression days. Work ethic was the major character development induced by my parents. Girls were girls and boys were boys and the natural consequence was that they would mix. Being raised on a farm wasn't conducive to wild social meetings so all through my school days the opportunity was very scarce and I was not the swiftest boy around girls, although I had a very strong and active libido. I never had a date through high school, but did like girls and got along with them well.

After graduation, making a living was more or less thrust upon me—by virtue of the farm being thrust upon me when I was 16. A continuation of that course was automatic and for five years I worked with little social outing, until the draft of 1950. My world turned 180 degrees in the army. Women and sex were the topic in most conversations, with eating and staying alive a distant second.

Needless to say, I came out of the army with a much broader view and perspective, but with not much experience. I married the first woman I ever had a date with. She really liked me and tried her very best to be a good mate. I reciprocated, I believe, to her satisfaction. Our personalities were just not compatible, which would have been very evident had we spent more time together before marriage. She was ready for nesting and I was too dumb to know what love was, or how a woman should be. That's what dating, going steady, and engagements are for—not just going to bed. Our first half dozen years were not bad, but a period of transition for me.

From milking cows to moving furniture, to selling food plans, to selling a bookkeeping service, to winding up selling real estate, which I grasped with all my unexposed, till then, ability. I found my niche in life and stayed with it for 50 years. This rambling prologue is my attempt to frame the picture, to explain how a seemingly unordinary development can progress one stage to the next, with no apparent recognition of the incongruity of it all.

My marriage was not a disaster. She did her duty as a mother to three kids and as a wife to a struggling husband, making a living in a world much different than he had been prepared for in his early celibate life. It was that very different world that I awakened to that made me realize that all was not well.

When I started my selling career, I soon realized that there were men and there were women, and they were different. And women could be just as predatory as men. There are women who want to get laid and use their feminine power to get there. I have always had a deep conviction that vows were to be kept, and I never forgot those marriage vows, and there were many times the opportunity was presented. But my case to point is Lucille, very much a woman, a personal friend. She is the very example of my whole thesis herein. She was 21 years older: She 54 and me 33. In fact, I went to high school with her daughter, one year older than I.

I met and knew Lucille the first time when I changed real estate offices and she had just started in the business. Her husband had died suddenly of a heart attack eight years previous and she was just getting back to living. We hit it off immediately. She had no men attachments and we quickly became friends. She was a very feminine woman but also very inde- pendent. She laughed a lot, could say dammit, loved to hear and tell raucous jokes and sex innuendos. Now here's the point of all this: Although we had private intercourse of banter, we did not have sex. When we first met, I had a wife and three kids, and I thought any married man who messed around was a horse's ass.

But I became aware of a lot in my marriage that was lack- ing. And living with a woman like Lucille could be much more than what I had. I was also becoming more aware of her increased intimacy which culminated in her setting up a se- duction opportunity which I declined (to this day, I believe I didn't do that right). We continued our business association and personal relations for 30 years, with her being the witness in my second marriage (after my five-year courtship). Rather than her coming to work for me when she changed offices and I became a broker, I advised her to go to another office, which had a good reputation, which she did. I bought my fifty-five- acre North Howell farm through her and her office, so our business relationship continued. She had a non-consummat- ed affair with a man who died. She was one of two women who were the best friends of my whole life who I didn't touch—but maybe should have.

HARLAN

In retrospect, Harlan Conkey was my first client who was neither a prior friend or family, nor connected in any way. He was a real estate investor who used me and respected my proficiency in the real estate business. To this day, I'm not sure whether I was a personal friend or a business friend, but he was a friend with a very intelligent, pleasant wife, Judy. His profession was audiologist, and she a professor at Monmouth Oregon College of Education (OCE). Their circle of friends included many connected to Oregon State College and OCE, with whom Harlan formed a small investor's group, with me being the broker for the group. He respected the little man, being the "slumlord of Monmouth." His reply: "They've got to have someplace to live and afford."

His little mobile park of travel trailers and campers wasn't high class but functional and a needed community. Blue-collar, beer-drinking, hardluck people needing their place to live. He and Judy lived in a 4,000 square foot home on top of a 40-acre field with a swimming pool. Harlan could always gauge the status of anyone he dealt with and talk to them on their level: Rich or poor, dumb or smart. He never blamed anyone for his mistakes; when one deal we made didn't turn out well, I indicated to him I should have been more observant and he laughed, "Dave, I'm a big boy over 21."

My introduction to the big time was when he was lured by Bill Austin, founder of Starky Hearing Aids, to come to work for him in Minneapolis, Minnesota, as CEO. Harlan decided they needed a factory in Portland, and asked me to find him one within close vicinity to the airport. I spent much time and was lucky enough to find exactly what they were looking for. A vacant building owned by Carl Polad, a billionaire banker in Indianapolis, where Starky had their main office, and was a man Bill Austin knew personally.

Harlan moved to Quebec where Starky had a factory, living in a condo there. He flew all over the world, starting factories in Europe, Australia, Texas, and Canada; and I believed they became the largest hearing aid company in the world. If I have one observation—looking back—it would be: I thought too small. When he and Austin wanted Palm Springs, I came up with a million dollar place, and he wound up buying another for 5 million dollars. When he wanted a pleasure yacht to entertain clients on the Columbia River, I was thinking 40 feet and they were thinking 140 feet. I drove a Mercury, they drove a Mercedes. All his high stress got to him when he was probably 55 years old. Open heart surgery—he had to slow down. As did I. We lost contact, and I just re-established contact with him. He is now living in Brownsville, Texas.

BILL

B ill and I met at breakfast sometime in 1974, a meeting ar-
ranged by Wally Satern, who I believe went to school with
Bill in Silverton. Wally always said he believed we should get
together, we kinda thought alike. He was right, and as Bill had
the innate ability to do, we hit it off immediately. That man,
put in the right environment, could have been a politician
of the highest caliber. His weakness, I believe, was thinking
that his Tom Sawyer, "Oh shucks" (and bib overalls) actually threw people off the track. It was obvious at first encounter with Bill that here was one smart son-of-a-bitch. He knew
where he was going, and he knew how to get there. He used
that "just fell off the turnip truck" image to it's highest degree,
but he was shrewd, shrewd, shrewd. I can safely say that, in
my looking at his associates, they were selected by Bill, and
in that sureness, I can take some satisfaction and pride in the
fact that he accepted me as the best real estate man to do the
job. I was among his group of friends including Ken Sherman
for his attorney, Tom Paulus as loan and money source, Kent
Aldridge as political power (he became mayor), and others;
but all part of a complete confederate of friends to help in the
final goal of complete success.

Don't think for a minute that Bill didn't know in the back
of his head "who can help me and who is irrelevant." We had
the partnership "Delko Development," and one of our first
partnership decisions was to have dinner together with our
wives at least once a month, which we did for as long as he
was married to Betty, and a few times with Louise. During all
this period our goals were the same and we used each other.
The difference was, I used his ideas and his aspirations, and
he used my knowledge and real estate experience to make

Delko a success. I was satisfied to work within the structure of our partnership, which wasn't encompassing enough for Bill. When he expanded his vision to Croisan Mountain, I bowed out, and he set his sights above Dave Delapp to Ron Jones, a big developer, who has name and prestige himself. I don't know the monetary outcome of Croisan Mountain, but Jones never gave up control; Bill probably did alright, but not as he hoped. It was at this time Delko Development began to lose focus, and in the early '90's, after selling Kennedy Mobile Home Park, which we had started and developed, we called it off, and Bill continued his set course. Our separation was like any other divorce: rancor, hard feelings, and discommunication.

As will happen with handshake agreements and partnerships, vision can be clouded by the "root of all evil:" Money. We had been in expansion and development mode with Delko up until the time Bill got a judgement against him for $140,000 by the IRS, in which they tied up everything he had his name on. I became immediately vulnerable to this foreclosure threat and was forced to sell the only property we owned that could generate the $140,000 cash in a short time (i.e. Kennedy MHP). When the time came for settlement, he paid his IRS and I claimed like amount for my share. Bill was into Croisan taking all his money, so he wanted to take more than his share of our sale, saying he put more into it. So began the conflict.

I suggested in lieu of court we seek arbitration which was provided by Willamette University through their legal department. We both assessed our contributions to Delko to submit to the arbitrator. Before the hearing got underway, I made the request that this arbitration was to be final. That win, lose, or draw; whatever he decided, we both, in writing, agreed to abide by it (I had been very upset and worried by all that turned a close relationship to, in my mind, being blatantly screwed by this partner, and I was definitely going to put an end to it).

The mediator had a prepared paper for us to sign just for this very thing. I signed it and shoved it over to Bill and looked him right in the eye and, without saying a word, I was saying, "Alright old boy, put up or shut up, no more dancing, put your name on the line." He did. We submitted our papers to the mediator and the next morning I received a letter from Bill's attorney. Instead of arbitration it became a legal matter in which of course he wanted to rescind the arbitration agreement he had signed. At the subsequent meeting with him and his lawyer, and Mark and I, we told him to abide by what he said or we go to court.

I had received the final payment on the MHP and I froze that in the bank. I took a whole week figuring out what we both had put in, plus labor and sales fees I had deferred, drew up a settlement statement with all figures, and handed it to him saying, this is the way it's going to be, say yes or no. I took a substantial hit, but had to get over it. He took it. We still had property sold on contract, which eventually worked out good, split 50–50.

As an analogue: I moved my office in 1997 to our Lyons home, so all communication with Bill and his doing unto others had ceased—until I stopped to get my Christmas tree from Jack Koch, our neighbor. He said, "Well, this is the last year for Christmas trees, I'm developing these 20 acres into a MHP." I said, "Who are you doing that with," and he floored me with, "Some guy named Bill." I said, "Jack, I know that man, and keep your butt covered, he'll give you that good old-boy honesty look and have his hand in your pocket. Bill doesn't have any money and he'll use your land to finance the whole thing."

Within the next two or three years, my nephew, who knew Jack as his teacher in FFA, said, "Jack is taking out bankruptcy." I went to see him and the first thing he said was, "I wish I had taken your advice, that crook took my land, fouled up the construction, took $40,000 up front for his consulting, ran the developement so far over budget we couldn't pay the bill, and we're being foreclosed out of the whole thing." He had to move to a little house and had a stroke. Someone took over the mortgage and converted it to a mobile home subdivision, and sold mobiles with lots.

This all took place at the same time Bill was finishing with Croisan and was working on Gibson Creek. The way he was operating, no one knew if he was rich or poor. There were a lot of people at Bill's funeral, including the first wife he divorced, who told my wife early in the game, "I hope Dave doesn't get taken in." A few of us didn't.

TOM CAMPBELL

There are six billion populating this world and no two people alike. There for sure was only one (Tom Campbell) in six billion. To be a friend of Tom you had to know how to laugh. Life for him wasn't always easy, but he made it fun. I had some influence on his business, but never sold him anything, but showed him many deals he bought. He made his own decisions when presented with the honest facts. I stress honest; he respected honesty and vilified anyone who wasn't honest. Our friendship culminated in our annual Alaska fishing trips during the last years of his life.

Our fishing trips were something that would never make "Fishing the West," but it sure would have made "Comedy Hour." We finally did get a good guide named Mike and, as Tom said, "We sure did break him in right." Mike referred to us as the *Oregon Odd Couple*: Tom being Catholic—me being Protestant, him being Democrat—me being Republican, he early to bed and early to rise—and me being late both ways. And, he never let me forget, he caught the biggest #75 King, a "wall hanger."

There are many stories about those trips that only he and I could recall with mutual laughter. The two that I've heard him repeat most often are two minor happenings that only Tom could elaborate with his gusto.

#1: We had gotten up early, fished until noon, and taken our fish to be processed, so that we were eating a big meal at about 2 o'clock. After the entrée I said, "I'll have pie and ice cream and a cup of coffee." This big, rather stout Swede waitress brought my dessert and set it down without a smile or a comment. Well, Alaska has refrigeration problems in the summer, so when she came by our booth and asked, "How was that?" I said, "Well, if the ice cream was as cold as the coffee, it would be fine." She bustled off in a huff, at which time Tom says, "DeLapp, let's get out of here before you get us killed." Of course, in his re-telling of this, she got bigger and meaner, but he nevertheless had never forgotten, even years later.

Incident #2 is the car. He always insisted I make all reservations, including renting a car in Anchorage, to drive down to the Kenai peninsula. I always kept in mind to shop for the best deals on air fare, lodging, guides, etc. So I reserved a car. As Tom recounted, "I stood on the curb with all our baggage and here comes this little sub-compact 2-door, and I says, "Well, there comes DeLapp with our car," and from then on he never stopped.

"Where's the pedals to make this thing go?"

"If we catch a big fish, we'll have to cut it in half and make two trips."

"Don't worry about hitting a moose, any one of them can outrun us."

"It should get good gas mileage; the Briggs Stratton engine starts with a pull rope."

The next year he called and said, "Make our reservations, and, DeLapp, get a bigger car." From the first trip until the last, he was a willing partner. Maybe only a small part of his life, but I've always felt very lucky to have been that part of it.

First Fishing Trip with Tom Campbell

Tom had lost his wife the year before so he needed to get
away, and I hadn't, so I needed the same thing.

I had made reservations to go salmon and halibut fishing with a guide. The blue rocket powered us to Ninilchick, on Cook Inlet, in good time. We met our guide and were launched by 6 a.m. with our foul weather gear, insulated and looking like moon walkers, but we were warm. As well known by all fisherman, fish are never where you put the boat in. You always have to go like a guided missile for at least a half hour and get to a place that looks exactly like where you were before. Although the guide said how good the water looked, how the tide was just right, how yesterday had been great, no one was more surprised than he when, within 30 minutes, I hooked a King. He completely lost his composure and things turned into a Chinese fire drill. Pole up, let her run! Get the engines up! Keep the other boats away! Where's the net! And God, Dave, you've got a wall hanger! What's more surprising was that I landed it, put it in the boat, and it did weigh 44 pounds. Not being bashful, I suggested that my partner might take a few pointers and quit teaching his Herring how to swim and catch something other than a cold. He maintained the one I caught was sick and with poor eyesight. That proved to be all the salmon action for that tide, so we pulled in and, like a scud missile, headed to the halibut grounds.

Halibut fishing is something else. Catching a halibut has all the excitement of watching a snail race. Let the bait down 100 feet, hit bottom, get a strike, reel up, throw the little ones (less than 25 lbs) back, and repeat for about three hours. I mentioned that there was an electric reel made for this which was laughed at and thoroughly ridiculed. But on the way back to sack out that afternoon, Tom asked, "Where is that guy with the power reel?" We were about to rent one for the next day, but the wind blew us off the water and it was arm-strong for the rest of the time.

We fished the Cook Inlet for about four days, then across the peninsula to Seward. Although for that day we had a different guide, the drill was still the same. Huddle in his open boat, going like someone was chasing us, for an hour to get where the Silvers were. The young guy knew where to go and, although it rained on us all day, we caught six salmon apiece. While hooking the first salmon, my line broke. The second salmon, the line broke. On the third one, the young guide says, "If this line breaks I'm jumping overboard," and Tom says, "If this one breaks you won't have to jump."

The other experiences, hooking something I never landed because it was too big, stopping along the road to take pictures of a big moose—because it was 20 feet away, hauling our fish in the little rented sub-compact ("one more fish and we'd have to be towed"), all completed the pleasure. We flew back with at least 150 pounds of salmon and halibut filets apiece. When I left Tom at his place, his parting shot was, "next time, DeLapp, I'll rent the car."

MY LAWYER FRIEND AND CLIENT
After showing him our home on the river

Sam:

It was with great perspicacity that I endeavored add to your quality of life, with peaceful repose by a Thoreau environment, to to find you have, without my expertise in the field of real estate, taken it upon yourself to acquire property by yourself. As implausible as this may seem, I can accept your protracted independence and can only suggest we further advance the cause by having dinner someplace they won't know us. I will suggest Stone Cliff, at Carver on the Clackamas River. It was dark when we ate there last but all swore there was a river below so we should probably try it in the daylight. The meal was good, ambiance great (a beautiful big log building)—you've probably eaten there, but that's alright, I didn't mention your name, they will let us come back. Any evening is good or, we are kinda Sunday afternoon dinner people, so make your decision, we're easy.

Dave

RAUL
My Honduran helper who became a good friend

When anybody says the name Raul Gonzales, I immediately conjure up the Mexican worker with seven kids picking fruit. When I met Raul, he immediately erased that pre-conceived and social, ethnic imprint. Here was a handsome, good looking man with sparkling eyes, a laughing smile, that showed a perfect set of white teeth that had never had a filling. This little man was genuine and showed it without even speaking. He had come to me. I had asked a friend who remodels rental houses, "Who did your work?" And he said, "Raul. And he can do it all. I'll send him to you because I'd like to keep him in the area." He showed up at my old house I had just bought. I asked, "When can you start?" And he said, "Right now. I have my tools with me." I then asked him, "How much do you charge?" And he replied, "Tom had been paying me $10 per hour." I said, "If you are only worth $10 per hour, I can't use you." Here was a man who had for all his life been told what he would be paid now being told he was worth more. I said what I needed done was worth $15 an hour if you do it right and stay on the job steady. I also realized that he lived 30 miles away and gas was $3.00 per gallon. He went to work immediately and within the first hour, I knew he was worth every nickel. Raul was married with two daughters and a grandson; he didn't smoke or drink, belonged to the Spanish church in North Salem, and was a technically experienced man in anything that needed done without close supervision. Tell him what you needed done and it was, "I do, no problem."

He was born and raised in Honduras, lived in Southern California, and came to Salem 11 years ago. He murdered the English language but always laughed at me when I had him repeat what he had just said. We became personal friends to the extent that I had him and his family up one Sunday for a BBQ on my deck. He was doing a good job for me and I was paying him $600 a week. When he had worked a couple of weeks he said, "The bank is selling my house and I have to find someplace to move." He had purchased a property unknowing the details of the deal at all. Two barracuda women, real estate brokers, had sold him a house at $145,000 that needed major work. The tax valuation was $58,000. They had a fraudulent appraisal of $145,000 and got a 100% financing with two mortgages of 80% and 20% with the seller paying all the costs.

So, Raul moved in without paying a dollar. The downside was that the payment was $1,100 a month, and after the first payment that he missed, it went to $1,500 a month, and foreclosure. It was the old scheme of everybody selling and making the commission with the payments unreal. I said to Raul, "Bring me your papers," and found the mortgage scheme was blatantly taking advantage of his ignorance. With a foreclosure sale without a judicial ruling, I called the mortgage company and said I'd been in business for 45 years, knew that they couldn't do what they intended to do, and they stopped the sale. I told him then not to pay another payment and so he lived there for another two years free until they did it right and did the foreclosure.

It is interesting that I wrote the mortgage company as an advisor for Raul, stating he would like to live there and you can settle this dilemma by re-doing the mortgage for $100,000 at 6%, 30 year amortization with $650 payments that he could make. I sent it registered mail and they received it, but never ever responded and ended up selling the property for $64,000. When he knew he was going to have to move he started looking for something to buy and found a single wide, two bedroom mobile home in Kennedy mobile home park. The park owners had taken this single wide for non-payment of rent. It is irrelevant but interesting that Kennedy Mobile Home Park was developed by me and a partner 25 years previous and was also occupied 85% by Mexican families. This home was vacant and condemned and they sold it for $1,500. Raul says, "I fix, make like new." I said, "Get three months free space rent while you fix it, and asked him, "Do you have the title?" "No, owners in California have it." I said, "Raul, you have to get the title before you can sell it." He said, "Manager says two weeks."

This went on for six months without the manager producing the title. Raul moved in and here's the critical element to this whole event. The park has a very detailed and complete application form oriented to the Spanish residents (i.e. citizenship, green card, work permits, etc.) which Raul had to produce when he moved in. He finished the rehab and said, "I need a bigger house for my family, and I found a double-wide for $21,500, and I can sell this one for $10,000 to the brother of a tenant." I went and looked at the double wide and said that I would finance this and take Raul's mobile home and sell it. When finishing the counter top one Friday morning, two deportation agents from ICE came where he was working, put him in handcuffs and shipped him to the center in Tacoma, Washington.

Eleven years prior, when he was in Southern California, he was cited to appear for a hearing of a minor infraction, but he was afraid they were going to deport him, so he didn't appear and immediately had a warrant issued for him (probably that's why he came to Salem). When I made the deal to take his trade, I instructed his daughter to get the title and do not take no for an answer, which she did. I then started the futile effort to save him. Lawyers, church, Senators, and they all said that you're wasting your time. Raul called me several times and finally said he had met some inmates who had been held there for a year. He did not want to do this and would rather go back to Honduras where his brother and dad lived. They deported him, and his wife and daughter still live here. He was set up.

When I sold the mobile home for $10,000, the couple who bought it were denied application to the park. The manager in a very revealing statement said, "You can't sell that without my consent, you're not going to live here." It was then that I realized that the agents knew where Raul was that Friday morning. The manager had his title and knew from his application that he was illegal, turning him in, knowing she could sell the mobile home for $10,000, and if I hadn't stepped in, she would have done it. I immediately hired a lawyer to write the owners of the park a letter, threatening them with a lawsuit. The owners of the park immediately came up, fired the old manager, hired a new one, and immediately accepted my new buyers. I am staying in contact with Raul in Honduras. His wife and daughters are living very comfortably in their new home and make me a payment promptly every month. He keeps inviting me to Honduras, which someday I may take him up on.

LETTER OF MY ATTORNEY

Owners of Kennedy Meadows

I represent a couple with a small baby who wish to reside in your mobile home park and have been denied occupancy by your managers. We feel you need to be aware of the extinuating circumstances to maybe avoid legal action. In 2011 you sold Raul Gonzales an abandoned mobile home at 2067 Kennedy Circle with conditions of rehab which he agreed to do to make it habitable. Raul is a very creative individual who did more improvement to the home than was required and made it worth $10,000. With 2 daughters, a wife and a grandson, he needed a larger home which he found in June 2013. One of the steady employers of his for the previous three years was Dave DeLapp who not only had Raul work for him, but became close friends. Mr. DeLapp helped finance the purchase of your Kennedy home and when Raul needed financing on the larger home he made the bargain with him to take the Kennedy home in exchange, leaving Raul with one space payment. This was done and then something unforeseen happened.

A Friday morning immigration authorities (at someone's direction) seized Raul at the Kennedy address where he happened to be that day and took him to Tacoma for deportation on a charge 12 years old. Raul was a devout family man, active in his church, neither smoked or drank, and the most dependable workman Mr. DeLapp had ever had and whom Mr. DeLapp had recommended to do work for his developer son and several other friends. Over the previous years Mr. DeLapp had discerned from Raul you had never given him title to the home and kept urging him to get it.

The manager kept making him promises "within the next two weeks." With his seizure Mr. DeLapp emphatically asked his wife to go get the title and the manager had it all the time, "Had lost it."

With Title, Mr. DeLapp sold the home (to the brother of a tenant in the park) with good work history, with a wife and new baby, who made it known they wanted to buy as soon as finished (new ceramic countertops, etc). When the new buyers made application for park tenancy, your manager denied it. It is Mr. DeLapp's contention that Raul was set up. Without the Title, his wife would be unable to sell the home and couldn't afford two space rents and the park would again have the home and title and buyers ready to buy a virtually new mobile home for ten thousand dollars. So any buyer DeLapp may have will be denied.

HANNAH

The girl with the laughing eyes

We go through this life in a hurry taking comfort and satisfaction in doing unto others and taking thanks when it is due. But how many times have we done some deed or said a favorable comment or made a suggestion for which we neither received any thank you, or for that matter, never expected any, and later learn it has had a profound effect on the person to whom it was offered. We don't always know what we have left in this old path of life—junk or jewels. This casual suggestion was a real life jewel.

When I mentioned to Marilyn, writing class mentor, that I had accumulated a stack of mostly undecipherable scribbling over the past 45 years, she said, "I would like to read some of it." When I then said I would like to put it all in book form and needed help to separate the grain from the chaff she agreed and said, "I know someone with that experience who would make a good match for you." She was so right. I wasn't quite prepared to meet Hannah, this vivacious 35-year old single woman who I hired immediately on our first handshake. Hannah is the perfect example of a "free spirit," that until then, I had had very little experience with. When out of high school at eighteen, she went alone to Zimbabwe, Africa (where she still has close friends), then to England for six years working on writing projects, and now returning to Mill City, her home town.

With infectious smile, and laughing eyes, I fell in love with her the second day of work, which to my chagrin is only three hours once a week. Besides being pretty she seems to have as much fun putting together my erratic memoirs as I do, and she types 75 words per minute, so my family book is taking shape, and I am enjoying it twice. There are some kernels amidst the chaff. As a second venture Hannah is doing a home dinner delivery business and brings me dinner twice a week.

So as a conclusion to my profound observation of seemingly innocuous comment by Marilyn, the path you leave behind in your worthless old life may have been strewn with jewels along with the junk. You may have enriched someone's life far beyond your wildest dream.

10

TRIPS AND ADVENTURES

FLOAT TRIP

I'm sure when my kids were growing up I probably made promises to go somewhere and didn't follow through on it, so when I said we could build a raft and float down the river all weekend they thought, sure! When? Well, I HAD A PLAN.

I had bought six truck inner tubes, picked out 2×4s and took three sheets of 4×8 plywood from my construction site and said, "Kids, get your sleeping bags ready for a weekend campout. We are going to take this weekend off and float down the river." On a beautiful Saturday morning we loaded all our gear into the pickup with the makings of a raft, went to West Salem under the bridge and nailed three 12-foot 2×4s together with 4×4 foot cross joists, making a frame 8×12 with six compartments each holding an inner tube. After nailing the three sheets of plywood onto the frame we had one of the neatest unsinkable rafts ever built.

The boys could not believe we were actually going to do it. We loaded all our food and eating utensils on, along with sleeping bags to sleep out overnight, waved their mother good-bye, telling her we would wind up in Newberg, and shoved off. I didn't tell them, but I hadn't the slightest idea how long it would take to get to Newberg. All I knew for positive was that it was downstream, and God knows we were going to float downstream. Of course every boater and water skier on the river came by to see what in the hell we were doing and to make a wake trying to swamp us, but the "David L" took it like a duck floating on top. The current from Salem past Keizer is pretty swift, so we were pretty far down the river in a couple of hours, thoroughly enjoying the whole scene, when what to my wayfaring eyes should appear but the Sheriff, star, gun, powerboat, and his nautical handbook.

"Do you have a permit for your raft?" he asked. "Anything floating on the water is a vessel, and a vessel must have a license or a permit."

"Well, all I got is two boys, plywood and inner tubes floating down the Willamette river," I said.

"Where are your life preservers? Every vessel must have one for each occupant."

"Well first of all," I replied, "I thought this was a raft with six life preserver inner tubes as flotation devices, which is two for each occupant."

"And, you must have life vests."

"Well, alright we are going to camp tonight on Grand Island at my friend's landing, Harvey Muyskins. I will call my wife to bring us life vests to save our life."

The sheriff bought this, left us, and never saw us again. Of course I had no idea where Harvey lived, never stopped on his property, never got life preservers, and continued our leisurely trip to the Wheatland Ferry. I believe the boys were having a ball, as was I.

I'm sure that Marion County Sheriff was glad when we floated out of his county. We camped out that night with sleeping bags on the river bank. Jay caught a fish (sucker) and Mark swam. We had snacks to eat and drink and all was quiet and peaceful, but the captain was a little apprehensive about our progress time-wise. When the river ran shallow we moved right along but when it deepened, there was very slow movement reaching St. Paul it was in the afternoon. We were not moving very fast and it looked like our ETA in Newberg was going to be after dark. Of course every powerboat on the river passed us 40 miles an hour and the stress on the engineering of our vessel was beginning to tell (i.e. it was coming apart about three miles to Newberg).

The river flows very slow, and at that time a man and woman pulled up to us to revel in our Tom Sawyer adventure. I took the opportunity and said, "How about you tow us to the landing." They were drunk and estatic, so we tied a rope to the front cross member and they promptly pulled off. I said, "Leave it here on the bank, take us to the landing and I'll come get it tomorrow."

So ended the trip, with wife picking us up at the boat launch at Newberg as planned. We had beached our vessel on the edge of a bean field. I retrieved it Monday and have the happy memories of an adventure we'll never forget.

THE DAY AFTER THE BEGINNING: 1969

A remembrance of Cheathams trip 1968
Farm friends from Illinois

Traditionally, New Year's Eve is the time of reflection on the past year. We do this by looking at movies taken in the past and clearly the highlight of '68 was the "Teton Trip" with your gang. The picture process is very incomplete, but it does act as the catalyst for our memories to fill the rest. For all the mountains, lakes, and rivers; bears, beavers, and geysers; people, towns and highways that we saw, all would have been insignificant if we hadn't been seeing it together with those who have fundamentally the same likes, philosophy, humor and problems, and people who are downright easy to like.

This time of year emphasizes two facts: (1) things don't make people happy. People make people happy. (2) whether it be presents or just enjoyment, it is much nicer to give than to receive. So if we gave any part of the enjoyment to you that we received, then that makes our togetherness that much better. It is nice to know that we could have a picnic with you in the middle of the Sahara Dessert and have a GOOD time, and one to remember.

Let's do it again! I ran across these snaps of the dry landers with their big expensive ocean-going fish and am sure you would like to have them.

D.L.D.

(The thoughts expressed above are the sole property of the management and reprint or broadcast is prohibited).

$450 FISHING TRIP

This little story will ring a bell with any fisherman and the luck that goes with it, bad and good. I raised three kids who are acceptable in a crowd, but the favorite presently could be the one whose friend Leo owns a B & B with fishing guide out of Grants Pass on the Rogue. Well, I'm from this real fishing area in the Canyon where the kids are taught the New Testament begins with Matthew, Mark, Luhr and Jensen; so when my son offered me a birthday trip of fishing on the Rogue, it took me 15 seconds to say, "Bake my cake, I'll be there tonight."

It is a beautiful spot; wonderful dinner (with birthday cake), nice cabin comfort, and up early to hit the water. Leo, the owner, says, "You two have the best guide on the river," and the guide says, "You get to be the first ones to try out this new super lightweight Graphite rod I just got yesterday for $450.00." Well, my highest amount had been $79.00 at GI Joe's, so success was guaranteed. I am somewhat handicapped with a few fingers missing on both hands, but I have landed a 96 pound Halibut and Kings on the Kenai River, so the Rogue was no problem. My son landed a keeper within 20 minutes and I got my unclipped throwback, so it started a beautiful day and continued all morning, with the guide continually bragging about his $450 outfits, and they were nice.

Late morning, drifting through his never-miss hole, my graphite double bent, a nice Chinook. I played him for awhile, like all professionals do and brought him up to the net when he made his last lunge for escape precisely at the same time I changed hands holding the rod. There went the rod, reel, hook, line, sinker and fish—and a large amount of dignity— to the bottom of the mighty Rogue. Unbelievably devastated, we all sat numb. All the guide could say over and over was, "I just paid $450 Saturday." My first thought was to throw him overboard and the second was to have my son cast into the hole, with no luck. The guide kept saying, "No use, there goes my four hundred fifty dollars," until I said, "It was all my fault, and I'll pay your damned four hundred and fifty dollars. In the meantime, I think I'll get sick and give up fishing for life."

Needless to say, that put a damper on the fishing for the rest of the day. We came home early, I wrote him a check with tears on it (he had to show me his receipt for $450, like I thought he was lying). That was a Tuesday. On Thursday afternoon Leo called and said, "I have some good news. We had four boats drift this morning and your guide told his story and told them where it all happened. The third boat through the hole snagged your line with his pole and pulled up the whole rig, rod, reel and lure so I tore up your check and hope your son brings you back for your birthday next year." I believe I'll go, but I'll tie the rig to the boat and use a rod for $29.

CHINOOK

I was born in Salem, the last of seven kids, 87 years ago. I grew up on several farms, went to Korea with a couple hundred thousand men to fight a war no one won and no one remembers, took two attempts at marriage, raised three kids, and through all those years did some fishing. The second marriage has lasted 40 years, and my real estate career has allowed me to wind up building my home and living these last 19 years on the banks of the Santiam—the most beautiful river in the US—and has made it possible to catch some big Kings in Alaska. The farm accident 29 years ago left me with just a thumb on my left hand and a thumb and two fingers on the right, so I figure that any fish I do catch, I'm giving them an even chance. I don't use the word retire, I can always think of one more deal to close and up until Saturday morning, September 12, 2015, one more big fish to catch.

I like Pacific City and caught my first steelhead on the Nestucca River 35 years ago. Two years ago, I ran into this guide, Tim Barnett, who took me on a drift from Beaver down the Nestucca to Cloverdale, just he and I. On that trip I caught the first winter steelhead of the year and had to release (which I cuss every time I have to do it). Tim Barnett knows the holes on that river from where we put in near Beaver all the way to the ocean and kept promising, "When the tide changes." Well that didn't happen to our benefit that day, but being on the water, a beautiful day and one helluva nice guide, who could not be happy?

Late August of this year I called him. He said, "I'm fishing the Columbia," and I said, "Fine, leave a seat open for me." I have caught fish on the Columbia and he said the 12th will be good. When I called him on the 6th of September he says,

"I'm switching to the Nehalem." On Friday he said, "Let's try the Nestucca, Saturday morning at six o'clock." Being a little disappointed to leave where he had been catching fish, I didn't know what God had planned for me but Tim says, "When the tide changes."

Well, I had heard that one before, but for the next two hours he got 12 nice crabs from crab pots that he put out. When the tide started coming in we were in the spot Tim wanted to be and we had two hits, and on the third pass through, "fish on" and I landed the third Chinook caught that morning of the 15 boats fishing, so at least I was going home with something besides crabs. My day was made, but Tim just said, "Now we get your second." One half hour later it happened: my pole bent double, the reel drag brake went *zziing* and I knew I had a big one.

Tim was a master in maneuvering the boat away from my line and I was clumsy as a cub bear with my two thumbs and two fingers; I was giving that big son-of-a-gun better than an even chance. We were able to drift out of the crowd of boats and after 30 minutes, that fish running all over the bay, he and I were both too tired to fight anymore, and Tim netted him on the opposite side of the boat out of my sight. With the exclamation "Dave, I don't think you should see this," he pulled that 50 -pound hog into the boat.

It's is the biggest salmon I have ever seen caught here in Oregon. It is one of those fish that every fisherman dreams about catching but probably the only fish that size caught on this river at least this year and I would think for the last several years. Henry Miller, fishing writer for *The Statesman* said he had only seen five salmon that size in the last 29 years. I'm taking him a picture. I left Tim that day saying "Well, if you want to put up with an 87-year-old man needing help getting in a boat without all his fingers, then I'll go with you again." He said, "If you can do that again, I'll take you." But I'm sure that that was just one of those once in a lifetime lucky happenings.

A GOOD BEGINNING

P.S. The sports writer for the Statesman paper wrote a nice article on the

"87-YEAR-OLD WITH FOUR FINGERS LANDING A WHOPPER"

with the follow-up next week saying:

"DeLapp got quite a bit of notoriety at the Senior Center and when asked his advice to fishermen, he said: "Have a good guide, use good equipment, new line, but you don't need to cut off six fingers."

A HAPPY ENDING

To Tim Barnett

Sometimes in the course of our everyday life we get the opportunity to enhance another's life and add to his enjoyment. I know you like to see one of your clients become friends and have a good experience fishing with you. Well, Saturday morning, the 12th of September, both happened for me. Hooking that big Chinook was not a problem and mostly luck, but landing him took some know-how, and I just want to thank you for your expertise. I am surprised by the number of people who saw the nice write-up Henry Miller gave us in the paper. I hope it did you some good, but maybe you don't need any more 87-year old feeble fishers. The Senior Center here in Stayton posted the paper on their bulletin board (which didn't make me a cent but was fun). Of course I got several copies from friends so if interested, I'll bring one our next trip.

Dave DeLapp

11

COMMUNITY THOUGHTS

COUNTRY ROAD ENGINEER

45849 River Loop Road
Lyons, OR 97358

January 23, 2001

Dear RiverLooper,

I know I may have taken the sport out of dodging potholes on River Loop, but they were getting so deep I think we lost a VW in the bottom of one. Anyway, I had a grader level the playing field and one load of gravel. Total cost to date is:

Gravel	$118.90
Grading	$60.00
TOTAL	$178.91

I think another load of gravel through the low area would be good for now. That brings the total to: $296.

For the 18 residents using this road, that amounts to: $16.44 each.

Now for you people who just said, "Well, we don't use all of River Loop, why should we pay?" You are the same people who eat the dust in the summer. So let's all co-operate and take care of that as well, and live right.

Let's get together before this summer. In the meantime, if taking care of the road was worth $16.50 to you, bring it to: Dave DeLapp, 45849 River Loop Rd. or drop it in the mail to P.O. Box 483, Lyons, OR 97358. Thank you for all your help in this matter.

Sincerely,
Dave DeLapp

SOME DO CARE

This is second of two letters to neighbors
(the letter I would like to mail).

Dear Riverloop Road Users,

To those of you who don't ride a horse to town anymore, you will realize our street problems have been worked out. The day of needing four-wheel drive to reach high ground is over. Of course, our first response was not, "Thanks and, who do we pay?" but rather, "You didn't do it right and I'm not going to pay." So for the benefit of you other cheap bastards: We saved you over $4,000 off the bid of a contractor for the same job. You have been driving on the road for 10 years without having to put a damned nickel, letting someone else buy gravel, use their tractor and blade, take their time. There have been some of you who have donated knowing there is no free lunch, and we thank you. Now for the rest of you bums, the free ride is over. We want $80 now ($8 a year for the past 10 years) and $100 a year (or $10 p/ month) from now on to maintain a road fund. If you don't want to do this, fine, move the hell out.

MOUNTAIN VIEW WESLEYAN CHURCH

I am Dave Delapp, the owner and landlord of 473 Clarmar Ave. in Salem. The tenants of this residence have been there for a couple of years. Jill Brewer and Lance Lyons have been friends as well as ideal tenants, taking care of my property. The past three or four months have been rough and I have been patient with their rent being late, and I believe they truly appreciated it. I have strong beliefs in helping those who need it, as you do, as witnessed by your check accompanying theirs for last months' rent.

More important than the money was the assurance that someone else believed in them and was ready to help. It was very gratifying to see what I believe should be the church's role in today's problems, not government's. In talking with your secretary, I got the distinct feeling you are doing good work. I also feel that the young people of today must face their responsibilities, and me forgiving payment of rent could send the wrong message, i.e. "this old man can afford it." With this in mind, I am returning your check so that you may use the money for more of your thoughtful benevolence. I will reiterate that I think your compassion for those who need a little help is to be commended. I will give them credit for the full month's rent being paid and hope they will repay you in some way for your help.

Fish Politics

On sending $50 to conservation organization

I am responding to your insert in today's Statesman. A few years back I attended an annual conference of Oregonians in Action, in which a biology professor from OSU gave a very convincing presentation on hatchery salmon as compared to native salmon, in which his thesis was that there is no difference and bureaucratic BS is destroying our fishing. He sold me and I have wanted to affect it in some way ever since. What a frustration to pay $25 to catch a salmon and throw him back (probably to die) because it wasn't fin clipped. I am retired with not a lot of fishing days left, but have some time to donate if I can help. I hope to get the names, some way, of those politicians who don't know a tadpole from a fishpole, and how to introduce the Oregon Fish and Game to use some common sense. The OIA can be a good partner politically. Yours truly, Dave DeLapp

MEMO TO THE CITY COUNCIL

Background: My wife Pat has volunteered helping one day a week at the Lyons Library for which she received a plaque for volunteer of the year. She wrote a memo to the mayor after unfounded condemnation of the library staff and assistants. The mayor called requesting a meeting with Pat in his office, in response to her note addressed to him about his criticism of the librarian and staff following a library board meeting. When going to the meeting, he had four other people to question and bully her about what she had written. So it was suggested by the volunteer help and library that she write this memo to the City Council because they need to know the interference this mayor created, which I then helped her to write.

Dear City Council: I have asked for permission to talk to you about a problem that I have observed for quite some time (nine years), that exists between this City Hall and the library. This has come to a head in the last few months, culminating in a final bullying of me in a meeting with the mayor and four other people, unannounced and me being unprepared for. I am aware that to settle the little petty squabbles isn't your duty, but the underlying issues are, and you gentlemen being the final authority must be made aware of the problem. Why me? Because I am a community volunteer who has enjoyed her use of public libraries for 40 years and I think I am a good help. This plaque verifies this to some degree as a volunteer for the CRB. I plan my week to be available every Wednesday afternoon to do the menial job the librarian delegates. There is always more to do than time allows. This library is a small facility but is a large part of this community. I have never been aware of any dissatisfaction with the service we provide and the extra effort given for all extra-curricular events.

Gentlemen, you cannot buy the kind of dedication exhibited in this library. That is why we were so dumbfounded to receive "the letter." Not just to the librarian but to all the staff. That rattled my cage. To receive such a diatribe the next day after a library board meeting which the mayor attended where issues were discussed and as we were thinking, settled. Upon seeing a memo from the mayor, I fully expected to read his commendation and maintenance of the library's duty and function through the physical personal problems of the librarian, instead, here was the militaristic edict of, "Do what I say, right or wrong." Well, I'm not paid to do a job and if the mayor or anyone else in this city hall doesn't appreciate it, I think it is my perogative to reply and I did. I didn't think my reply was so vicious as to warrant the bullying in the meeting. But evidently I hit a nerve and here we are.

What do I want? First of all, if you don't know anything about running a library and have no experience, keep the hell out of there and keep the people out of there when the librarian or assistant isn't there (this is in reference to the person who was not qualified to rearrange the library and disrupt the job of the librarian, and which caused distraction all the way around). #2 If you are interested and want to help, cooperate with us. We need file carts with lids to put sale books in or to store them, which can be handled with a hand truck without spreading them all over (I am donating storage space now). #3 we can train the interested school kids and adults to do more than just clean up and filing, even to help people use the computers. Free up Brenda and

Rosemary to attend to the discards. This is like our garage:
Never big enough, but some things can be eliminated. In
conclusion, this bickering between City Hall and library
started before this mayor. We have a good, efficient facility that God knows the community surely needs. I would
hope that you gentlemen would keep showing your interest
in it and advise against any further discouraging attitudes of
your employees.

P.S. One year later the mayor resigned.

THE ROADSIDE STAND

I am a peddler

I am a local product, born and raised in Oregon, mostly Salem. I believe in supporting the local economy. Having been a farmer locally in the past, my allegiance is to the farmer raising the crops which are recognized nationally as being the finest in the nation, and specifically, the Oregon strawberry grown here in the Willamette Valley. None is finer, yet the industry is failing and why? Today I purchased two pints of strawberries, 22 ounces in weight, for $4.00, or $2.90 a pound. Three weeks ago, I purchased California berries, four pounds for $5.00, or $1.25 per pound. Those berries were picked, packaged, shipped in one pound boxes and sold for half the price of local produce. An acre of strawberries' average is 10,000 pounds per acre. At $2.90 this computes to $29,000 per acre gross.

Of course, picking is high and expenses are high, but someone is gouging and the industry will die. So, no more lamenting the poor farmer who has to grow something else. He got greedy and priced himself out of the market. One other point is that a lot of people will U-pick, eliminating all expense of harvesting for the grower, only to find the cost higher than in the store. The average family cannot afford to support the local grower. They will buy berries grown in California and sold to Safeway rather than the local grower.

THE BET

When you have rentals and the toilet is stopped up, when the oven doesn't heat, when your furnace quits, it is always a problem between you and the renter. When the roof leaks, it is between you and God. He makes the rain but he doesn't fix roofs. So when Raul went up on the roof of my duplex to repair the skylights he says, "The roof is very bad." It being 30 years old this is no surprise to me. It's time to re-roof before it starts to leak. Raul says" I can do, I get help". So I bring in the dumpster, they tear off the old roof, put on new underlayment and I go to buy 3,600 feet of new three tab architectural 30 year composition roofing. Needing 108 bundles at $20–$25 a bundle, this is a sizable amount, so I did some shopping. The big box Home Depot says, we have a special on for $19.75 a bundle and the salesman gave me a print out sheet for the 36 squares necessary.

I don't own stock in Home Depot so think it only fair to give the local dealer a shot, so I drove out to Brooks to the big local dealer who does a lot of commercial roofing. The salesman at the counter figured out my price for $24.75 a bundle, to which I replied, "Your competition is five dollars cheaper." The owner setting at his desk overheard the conversation and said "no they're not", in a very positive no-argument tone, to which I took exception. He says, "No one beats our price by five dollars." I said back to him, "Well, you seem to be pretty sure about that," and he answered, "Yes, I am positive". That did raise my competitive spirit just a trifle so I did something that I had heard done but I had never done before. I said, "Well, I've got $100 in my pocket that says you're wrong," and he says, "You're on," thinking I had no way to backup my bet. I went out to the pickup, brought in the written bid with the same specs, with lower price, threw it on his desk and never said a word. He looked it all over, turned to the salesman who is witnessing all of this and said, "They got a deal with ABC," to which I replied, "I don't care if they got a deal with God himself, this is their price to me." He then reached in his desk drawer, took two $50 bills and threw them on the counter. I picked them up and walked out the door.

I'm sure more than one person driving by me said to himself, "I wonder what the silly guy in a red pickup is laughing to himself about." When I got back to my office I had just gotten a flyer from Union Gospel Mission for donations. I wrote them a check for a hundred dollars, made a copy of it and sent it to the owner of the roofing company saying, "You just bought 52 meals at the Union Gospel Mission and I'll take the donation with the write off."

Home Depot did deliver as they had promised and even made roof delivery. And I had estimated within a bundle and a half what I needed." Raul did a good job putting the roofing on, I saved $500 and had a roof on my duplex without ever having to worry about it raining. And I never knew I could have so much fun putting a new roof on a building.

12

POETRY

We Make Our Light

Brothers and sisters
how we love to meet and laugh and talk and brag and joke
but never cry except when another needs our soul
   to help him in his time of need
how bright we make the dark of any night
when for a time we light the world in which we live
    and to each other give
     the warmth of spirit, in each embued
    by some genetic grain that grows, renewed
     as though regenerated by souls
     that need the closeness of kind
and derived from a source reminded by us again
    as seen in the character of us all

No need to light a flame
   or turn the lamp to chase the gloom
    from any place
the energy we still ignite
could lighten the darkest night
the warmth could do away with any need of fire or heat
 for when we meet
    each one can add another spark
      and fan the flame of family love

More at Christmas than anytime
   we renew our inner light to shine
and like that string of Christmas lights
   only when the juice can flow through each
   does all the circuits close and all can glow
   so each is different of hue
      but necessary for all to light
      and make the tree of family bright.

So though we live and make our light
   and gather together to create a bright
    that lasts us each in our own life
let's pray we leave a genetic glow
   that when our kids do gather too
    that light – that spark – may carry through
   to help them through the darkest night
   and they for good will make their light.

by David Lee DeLapp
1991

RETIREMENT POEM

Once again comes the time
to put our year in nonsense rhyme.
It just wouldn't be Christmas unless a fool
Recounts their whole life in time for Yule.
Just the fact that we survived for another good year
Should be all that is needed to tell our good cheer.

Now that we are both in our eighties, and that's not degrees
A shot of Old Granddad is our needed antifreeze.
Driving still harmless, either lucky or no fear
In fact would've been perfect if not for that deer.
If we overlook our weight, hernia, bad eyes
Enlarged prostrate, glaucoma, no exercise;
Fake knees, cataracts and nearly deaf,
We can't complain, cause there's not too much left.

I finished a fix up project I bought in 0'10,
Sold it quickly, so maybe I'll do it again.
February weather makes one wishing for sun
So we flew to Kuaui for 2 weeks of fun.
Spent all our money, but one shining light,
The renters were still paying, so we rested at night.

Summer came on and another great feat
We're still married to each other, another years' treat;
So we went to Colorado, the Broadmoor Hotel,
Acted like we belonged and no one could tell
We were old retired folks enjoying the scenery
They smiled ear to ear, taking out greenery.

CHAPTER TWELVE

Went fishing twice, caught two big nice springers,
Not too bad for a man with only two fingers.

The kids are all healthy, grandkids the same
Behaving themselves the way they were trained.
There's more things to tell and to keep from repeating,
You should stop in and see us
And join us in eating.

A barbequed steak on the deck by the river
But don't wait too long, tho' we come from long livers.
The only things going fast are the days
With your caring and B.S.ing,
We'll stay happy always.

AFTERGLOW

How right it is to have a get together during the Christmas season. How like a string of Christmas lights—shining in our own way but needing the juice to flow through each one to make them all glow. How absolutely lucky can one family be. Just look at our string of lights and colors—what a tree (or maybe closer to a fruit cake)!

Consider the mix:

The sisters—one who makes cooking and eating an event, a way of life; another who can wisecrack at the drop of a hat; the next one whose love and talent for drama makes any conversation exciting; and the youngest sister whose artistic talent and originality is almost awesome.

The brothers—a mechanical spirit of depth and resource who could fix the world; the second a humorist with jokes flowing in his veins; the youngest a horse trader who deals and squeals.

How can these different people even begin to communicate? Somehow through all that varied personalities runs the thread of wit—humor—respect and good judgment of themselves and others. When Mom and Dad threw the dice they sure came up a lucky seven. Our family tree is shining bright.

A Merry Christmas Gift for Us

It's been a long time since my two boys
spent time with their Dad, and the joys
of fishes that are fighting
and bugs that are biting,
with a motor boat being the noise.

We've tried this year on the ocean
but there's something about all that motion
So let us partake
of calm Paulina Lake
and fish when they just take a notion.

We'll take our own bait
but the Lodge needs a date
(in the next 30 days)
to supply us with bed and food.
My time is my own,
so you two let it be known
when early summer we go for 2 or 3 nights in a row.

CALL ME

I regret to say no children allowed.

Two sons and Dad with boat stayed three nights, four days at
Paulina Lake the next summer.

To Norma

on putting my shorts in washing
with red clothing

What makes that man so austere
Hard to know, quite severe,
Even on the chilly side
In his friends, he'll not confide

Overnight he has assumed
A different look, and act presumed
To cover an unwanted load
A mental burden there abodes

From nonchalance to ruthlessness
Driving like a man possessed
Of disfigurement or some disease
Fearing recognition will displease

What changed his masculine confidence,
To one who now takes fast offense?
The answer is not what you may think,
It's simply that his shorts are pink.

13

FISH AND CHIPS

TO BOB THORBECK, A FRIEND ATTORNEY

Dear Mr. Thorbeck:

Nice hearing from you again. Hope the family is all well.
Now about that bill you sent me. Things down here on the
farm haven't gone too well. The horse got colic. Shep the dog
got heart worms. The ole ewe got liver fluke. My lumbago
has been something fierce, this wet weather. And of course
I'm sure you heard about the wife. My daughter, the eldest
child, married a city fellow last month, kind of fast and
sudden, but as she says, why wait?

Now Mr. Thorbeck, about the money I and another
fellow owe you. I had it figured out my hay money would
take care of it, but it got rained on. The other fellow lives
where the phone systems must not be too good, his phone is
always disconnected. I know I owe you, and when I get some
money, you know you are at the top of my list right next to
the hospital bill and electric company.

Things have got me down so low, I am taking off for the
rest of the week; that grandkid of mine just has to take his
grandpa fishing. It will do us both good. Give my best to the
little lady.

Dave

P.S. I am sending you this lottery ticket, maybe your luck is
better. I spent my last dollar trying.

Overt Observation

On one of our trips to Phoenix, Arizona to watch the Mariners play spring practice, we spent a couple of weeks and came home by the Grand Canyon. I had reservations to stay at the Grand Canyon Hotel which was very enjoyable. The next morning, on leaving, I said, "It's quite a ways to get gas so I have to fill up here at this high-priced gas station. I was driving my new Pontiac that we had only had for a couple years and so I blithely pulled into the right-hand side of the pumps. Of course it is self service. I got out, I ran my card through the little deal, was taking the nozzle out of the holder, when the man standing on the other side of the side of the island filling his motor home with gas (who didn't know Octane from October) just nonchalantly said, "Does that Pontiac use diesel?" I looked at the pump and sure enough I had come that close to filling my tank with diesel. I thanked him profusely and in fact shined his shoes and washed his windshield and said, "Hey, you saved me a lot of trouble," and I've often wondered since what would've happened had I filled my tank with diesel.

TO BROTHER-IN-LAW DEAN

on hearing he had been diagnosed with pancreatic cancer

Dean,

I know you are surprised at getting this but sometimes
surprises come from unexpected places. That makes this
event a surprise. The other thing is, more often than not,
it's sometimes that important things never get said in time
and some of the unimportant things, meaning little to just a
few, do get said. Your show of guts and your health problems
prompt me to write one of the very insignificant sides of my
book. A significant side of my story is when your mother was
living with us. I liked your mother. She could be a handful in
her mild senility but never unlovable. For instance, walking
into our bedroom one morning while we were, quote, "in
the act" didn't seem to affect her a bit. She just smiled and
left us, and I'm sure forgot what she had seen.

She was always up for riding with us in the pickup with
our pig Roxanne, your mom was as much fun as the trip,
singing little silly ditties, or quoting her favorite poem, that
I will review, and just generally having a good time. I don't
think she ever really got what we were doing hauling a big,
old, fat pig around, but she was always ready to go even
for just a ride out to the farm. So I'm sending this to you
to make your day different. It is one of the 75 in my book.
Forgettable, but not a waste of time. I'm having a good time
writing all these things. There are more if you are interested,
and I can certainly understand why not.

A THANK YOU TO CHRISCIA

A short time ago, a woman friend visiting us made the comment in kind of an oblique fashion, that at my age if there are any unsaid compliments or admiration, that perhaps I should be saying them. The comment was made when I casually said something about how well I thought Mark was doing. She said, "Have you told him how you feel?" I said, "I'm sure he knows," and she came out with, "You better be telling him before it's too late." So, that is an explanation for my note to Chriscia. First of all, thank you for your warm and gracious acceptance of our company in your home. I know it may be hard to believe, but I'm not too old to learn. And it was in our visitation that I learned something. That is the thesis of this whole note. You demonstrated the term 'deep convictions' more than anyone I've ever met. Your positive declaration of Heaven and Democrats can only make me hope you have the same convictions of me. In fact, I've given some thought to going to church and changing my vote to Democrat.

We all have known persons who have beliefs, not based on their own personal experience of thinking or teaching, that causes them to follow without reasoning. I hope you realize how much I did appreciate and enjoy your feelings. You are an unusually perceptive woman. I may not get baptized or start going to church but you have made a strong case by your positive conviction. Voting Democrat doesn't have the eternal effects but is still worth considering.

EARNING ACCOLADES
2012

To: Ken Sherman (lawyer friend for 50 years)

Dear Ken,

Just a note about your fish picture in this morning's *Statesman*. It occurred to me that you and I have progressed from our notable accomplishments in the last 50 years to, "Well, he's still alive." You've got a few years on me but we are holding up our end of the fishing, glad to see it (I've been with Trevor, nice guy, caught fish).

Dave DeLapp
On the river @Lyons

SANTIAM SYMPHONY

A lot of people live their lives anticipating the big happening, which most times doesn't happen and they miss the small things that make up most of our lives. I am a small time happening man. My son and Pam, his lady friend, bought a big painting from my sister which had to be hauled in a pickup. I offered to deliver it to them and when asked what time, I said, "How about around supper time?" They had a hard time refusing.

So in our after dinner wine drinking session, discussing world shaking events, Pam mentioned that the rain and leaves had made her deck slippery and very treacherous and said to me,

"You don't go out on your deck when when it is slick like that do you?" to which I replied,

"Yes, when I let the cat out at 10 o'clock at night, I pee off the deck into the bushes and you can't believe the rapture of relieving and hearing the steady roar of the river 30 feet away in the dark stillness of the night."

Mark then asks, " Does the noise of the river give you a little more distance?" to which I replied,

"I think quite a bit more arc." Pam added with typical female envy the 'how convenient your appendage is to obtain such enjoyment from a natural environment'.

I then gave them a bit of history trivia, of the first unknown explorer who witnessed the Grand Canyon and said from his standing on one projection, that he could pee for a mile. So it is with these observations of the significant events that make our life very interesting. This, mainly, is what life is all about.

GREENBAUM'S HELP

This is a letter of compliment to Greenbaum's Fabric Store. I am an old man by anyone's reference and I have voiced complaints of poor help and sometimes owners for some companies. This is the first to complement such help. You and I have been in business in Salem longer than we deserve but sometimes your reputation and reliability does survive. So when I wanted some wallpaper, I thought of Greenbaum's first. I was greeted in your store by this very pleasant woman. I can only assume she is an employee, if owner, only so much the better. If she is single and I was sixty years younger I would marry her tomorrow. Her genuineness, her friendly laugh, helpfulness and being pretty is far above average. I went in for wallpaper but felt like buying a yard of Pendleton material just to talk to her. Raise her wages if you're the owner, you can't miss.

When I was in business in Salem 30 years ago I hired a girl Julie, who after leaving me, went to work for Greenbaum's. She was also cute, personable and smart. We have maintained a friendship since that time. You must have a way to draw nice people. Please pass this on to the personable young lady who was so gracious to an old man. She suggested where to go for my wallpaper and I left feeling I just been given a free gift. As the much overused statement is, "She made my day."

Thank you.

A THANK YOU NOTE FOR $36,000 PAID IN THE PAST FIVE YEARS

April 29, 2013

Jennifer Knowlton

April Ct.

Dear Jennifer:

It isn't often that I have the opportunity to thank a tenant for 5 years of payments, and pleasant, honest relationship. Although my dependence on gut feeling has not been 100%, you have come through in flying colors, bolstering my judgment ability. Maybe your judgment has not been flawless, but your honesty is. When things were tough, you let know and more than that, when things were good, you paid in advance.

I wish you all the success in the next five years.

Dave

THE DECK IS STACKED

*This meeting was in Springfield with the two officers of the
mobile home tenants association*

August 25, 2013

Charlie Ricker,

My meeting with you and Rita was a very refreshing experience, in that I haven't been that involved in such real estate
decision for 20 years. It is good to feel I may contribute
some ideas that could help in formulating a positive solution, however most free advice is usually worth just that.

My first thought. Whomever is your most influential advocate in the legislative arena contact Oregonians in Action,
Dave Hunnicutt. They are very staunch advocates of real
estate owners rights and have their own attorney. I have no
idea how they will come down on this, but a strong presentation enlisting their help would give your cause a great boost.
They are very strong on owner property rights.

As Reagan said, "we can't look to governments to solve
our problems; the government is our problem." The laws as
they now exist give every right to the lessor. Those rights
have to be modified to effect rights of the lessee, to protect his rights of ownership. I have full conviction that a
long term land lease on placing a home would end the space
rent escalation as now allowed under "reasonable return
on investment clause," preventing any tenant reparation or
protest on space increase, and end speculation purchases of
parks based on no control, by law, of any regulated increase.
The park I built has increased the space rent 400 percent
since 1986 without one cent improvement or benefit to the
lessee. A long term lease would prevent this. This park was

designed and developed for modest cost homeowner living with no pool, club house, or extra communal expense.

My thought may not be of value. I'm thinking all individual homeowner associations should combine to a stronger state-wide organization with a spokesman with clout. We will get nowhere in little individual skirmishes to regulate dictatorial managers, that the law allows them the power they now have. I can assume my thoughts may have been considered before, and I am fully aware that I'm not the most brilliant player in the game, and old age doesn't necessarily cause smartness, but experience sometimes can be a plus. If you think I can be of any use I have plenty of free time now that I'm retired to offer any help or advice that you feel I might be able to help you with. Feel free to give me a call.

Dave DeLapp

Dear Mr. Sillwell:

Received final bankruptcy notice today, hope this gets you straightened out. I am writing this as a reminder to you in case you have filed me in with the other creditors. I gave you $11,500 in cold hard earned cash - it wasn't rent (although I gave you several thousand of that too) or phone service, or advertising or any of these service debts that cost just pennies on a dollar, but cold hard money that I invested and never got back. Although bankruptcy allows you to wipe the slate clean in most cases, it doesn't address the morality of the debt owed.

I can only have reasonable confidence that you appreciate what I tried to offer you, an opportunity to have a future in your own business

Dave DeLapp

My response to his two bills that I felt were gouging me:

Wally Lien
1775 32nd Pl. NE
Salem, OR 97303

July 25, 2013

Dear Mr. Lien:

I am sending two checks, leaving it up to your conscience whether to tear the second one up. (No) 1 added to your February payment is $1000, (No) 2 is for your statement of past due balance.

I stopped by your office three different times and you were there but too busy to talk to me, your contract didn't stipulate an appointment was necessary to talk to you. I could only conclude you hadn't done anything, which proved to be true, except charge me $600 for phone calls. I learned from other attorneys that the course you proposed to have a court set aside a ruling was impossible in the time frame we had been given to close the deal. This was evidently your final decision when you advised me to find another Title Co. That conclusion was not too brilliant. Wally, both you and I know you didn't do me a dimes worth of good. Let your conscience be your guide.

Dave DeLapp

P.S. Later – he cashed the lesser of the two.

ALL MY RENTERS WEREN'T HONEST

Sometimes forgiveness is hard to do. This one said her daughter was dying, then conned me out of six months rent at $3,000. This letter was a week before Christmas.

Dave-

I know you must be very mad and are planning to evict me. I'm begging you not to evict me. My taxes have been sent off and I will have them back in 5-10 business days. I will send you payment for Dec, Jan and February as soon as I get the money from my taxes. If you are so mad that I must move please just give me a 30 day notice and not an eviction. I won't be able to rent anywhere and I truly apologize for being so late. I haven't called because I felt bad and was worried what you would do and I was embarrassed. Again, I will be sending 3 months of rent in the next two weeks. And please don't evict me.

Thanks for listening,
Christine Newcity
473 Clarmar

14

THE LAST 87

THE FLY IN THE BOTTLE

Another one of my reflective moments

While I was sitting here at my desk Monday morning trying to figure out what immediate jobs I could get out of today, and which bills are past due, I was bothered by a fly buzzing around which ultimately landed on and crawled into a water bottle on my window sill with two inches of water in it. I said, "All right pest, I've got you," and put my thumb over the top and shook it vigorously several times thinking I'd drown the little obnoxious bastard. I reduced his flying ability but he continued living so I did it again more vibrantly. He did the breaststroke for another five minutes with his tenacious desire to live, so I did my experiment to see if he would recognize a lifeline. I took a short string and lowered it in to him in the water. He grabbed it immediately and climbed out of the bottle to safety. It took him 15 minutes of drying out, and climbing around the top of the bottle, up and down the string and finally flew away. Probably to find a horse turd to crawl on, or bat his head against another window, but he lived another day. At some times in our lives, we all can use a lifeline. We have to recognize it or drown.

If ever there is a case for the existence of a supreme force which we have labeled God, it would be within the desire of this insect to live. We have also labelled it as instinct. Regardless of the name, here's a living body with a brain so small it would take 1,000 to weigh an ounce. Yet, it has the capability to seize the opportunity given to him to live. As in humans, was the endowment stronger in this fly than in other flies? So, to extend the premise of supreme force, God, where does the soul become a factor of life and the hereafter or for that matter, the heretofore? Not many religions address the before, just the hereafter, augmented by this strong instinct to live. The profound reality is that every one of the trillions of living things, from ants to elephants, will exert this unbelievable act to live. We humans, with this extraordinary capability to wonder of our existence, have to invent some Higher Power, labelled whatever, to give meaning to that existence and to deny its ending.

90 Percent

This little scenario has been replayed in every household in the world. The old Iroquois chiefs may have had problems but it was also the trivial happenings of killing and skinning a buffalo, taking care of the pony that were part of life. But did he ever come home to the kitchen sink stopped up? I got home at 5:00 on a Monday with a meeting that night to the words, "The kitchen sink drain is leaking and I can't use the sink or the dishwasher!" Tuesday night, the dishes are accumulating so the pressure is on. Wednesday afternoon I tackle the job. With new drain parts installed, the sink won't drain. That was the problem in the first place.

Has anyone ever actually unstopped a plugged drain with Drain-O? Aren't all those products just something to do until the Roto-Rooter shows us? Isn't the Roto-Rooter just a cop-out for the home fixer? Didn't I work until midnight Wednesday night trying to unplug that damn drain, and with the promise of tomorrow we'll eat at home, I go to bed.

On Thursday, I approach the problem with several options I have worked on, all of which have the nagging, hidden feeling that Roto Rooter will be the final answer. But despite all this doubt and trepidation, I hooked the drain back up and ran water in the sink, turned on the disposal, and one of the ecclesiastical miracles, the water drains out. The Drain-O has worked. This may be one of life's small victories, but none is sweeter, and once again it is proven, 90% of your worries never happen.

Mondays

Mondays are always the start of new ideas—the beginning of some new phase of ideas that have formulated over the weekend. On Fridays I look forward to the weekends, but Mondays have the surprise awaiting for some new action. Maybe the first two hours are catching up any loose ends not finished Friday, but then, importantly, it is a day to initiate something. Who could start anything on Thursday or Friday? Too close to quitting time. A Monday night writing class makes that day come quickly, especially when that assignment isn't done. The story of my life is, Mondays come too fast but it is the day to start moving.

GOD AND I IN THE REAL ESTATE BUSINESS

I suppose, after all, if He created this big, round ball of rock and dirt, there would be no better partner. I bought this old house to remodel and He gave me His blessing, but it is taking my money to fix it. I tried prayer but the lumberyard wants money. I can only pray that He sends us a buyer with good credit. He contends He just created the dirt but the house repair is out of His hands and is now my problem. The bank said, *In God We Trust*, but you sign a note. God says the closest to owning a building are His outlets on prime locations open Sunday mornings and some Saturdays.

I am reminded of an exchange of real estate with a group who the general partner who had God on his side. We ended the resulting negotiations with a prayer. Well, evidently the general partner had used a little bit of God's and the investor's funds to buy a condo, so the State of Oregon wants to put him in the penitentiary for something called a Ponzi Scheme. He had to go to Texas to live where there is still God, but not strong laws or extradition. I learned later on that he relocated in Oregon, started this same scheme, and used some of the previous God-believing investors.

Another circumstance of divine participation was the Lutheran minister buying $200,000 of property, because my client was in another town and another county, he said, "My congregation doesn't need to be aware of my investing in this property." I often wondered if the congregation tithes to help save souls went for that purpose or maybe part of it went to re-roof his apartment houses.

I think I have hit on a pretty good deal. I keep on starting projects so that God keeps me well to finish it and I may never quit.

No One Knows
How Old Am I Today?

W ell, I really can't answer that. You see, I have been blessed with a clear mind that continually conjures up new and exciting thoughts and things to do. I have retained a very good sense of humor that not only makes other people laugh, but also amuses me. I enjoying eating good food, going to new places, and improving on those old habits I've always enjoyed. These things and many more keep me young, and the amazing thing, the pleasures are coming easier and more often, so I can only conclude that I must be getting younger every day. To measure age by years has always been other people's concept, not mine. If you want to know how many years since I was born, that I can you tell you. But how old am I? I am sure of only one thing—I'm much younger than anyone else born the same day.

Chip

LIFE TO LIVE NOW!!!

My New Year Resolution

▶ I believe inaction begets inaction. The less obligated I am to do, the less initiative I have to take.

▶ Time deadlines, for me, aren't that bad. If they aren't there, I let things go.

▶ But I am just becoming aware of how hard it is for me to finish things.

▶ In that same regard, I am constantly assuming positions that require follow-through, that I become inclined to let drift until either someone else must do it, or I'm forced by deadline to complete it myself.

▶ I'm aware that watching all these 'most interesting things on TV', is nothing more than an excuse for *failing to act.*

▶ *It's too cold outside,* is absolutely no excuse for not doing the things inside that need done.

▶ *'I'm retired'* and *'I'll do that when I feel like it'* is just another excuse that I use to justify sitting on my butt all day.

▶ So, the first thing I am doing is identifying those things that never got finished along with those things that never got started and those things I have made a commitment to do.

▶ In the next two weeks, I propose to do the following without pushing myself too hard . . .

REPUTATION

(Living up to or living down)

On Saturday, my son and I spent a beautiful February sunny afternoon watching a highly advertised Harlem Globetrotters exhibition basketball game in Portland's Rose Garden Center. They have been the iconic entertainers of the basketball world for over 80 years. After both agreeing we wasted a beautiful afternoon my son said, "They sure didn't live up to their reputation," which was my sole reason for ordering the tickets. I first saw them 70 years ago when I was in my teens and 50 years later when he was the same, and the Globetrotters were hungry and fun to watch.

In 1925 a Jewish promoter saw the potential in these Harlem ball handlers with their slapstick comedy routines and natural extraordinary physical impossibilities with a basketball. He formulated a brainstorming group of semi-pro black players and had them play professional teams, beating them regularly. Along with competitive play, they were coached to put on a show all over the world. What we saw Saturday was a raucous exhibition of average talent, blaring amplifiers, and too little demonstration of ability. The show had the phony atmosphere of professional wrestling and I don't like watching professional wrestling. Their act was very juvenile, not funny and an embarrassment. I'm sure Abe Saperstein was turning over in his grave.

I write of this as being what I see as the dumbing down of the general public and such is the task of living up to your reputation. If in our lives, we have started out being honest, working hard, striving to be liked and using our God-given abilities, doesn't that reputation remain with us? Doesn't that person with the shady background have to work like hell to

DAVE DELAPP — CHIPS

shake it? When we see someone who we know has established his own honored reputation, we recognize strength of character. When we witness shallow presentations of less, accepted as the norm, it is truly disheartening, to say the least.

My last comment about those that attended: They were not 86 years old. They hadn't seen the originals. They live in today's world where this is the norm and like the comparison to music of today and 60 years ago, I think we saw the best. May the public excuse my criticism of their acceptance of a fallen reputation.

ON THE DEATH OF NORMAN —
MY BROTHER'S OLDEST SON

Question Concerning Death
in Relation to the Christian Religion

N orman was a prime example of civilizations' ideal man. Raised in a religious moral family, he embodied every virtue everyone could hope for. At 29 years old he was suddenly taken from this world of the living by an accident working with his father late at night helping to repair an electric compressor at his uncle's farm. Such a meaningless tragedy can't help but make one question the religious belief espoused at the funeral, "This is his moment of glory. He was fully prepared to meet his maker." If a Christian is fully prepared, and this is his glorious moment, should he then look forward to the termination of his earthly existence? Isn't this really an unbalanced attitude? Isn't this the same as saying he should want to die? How is this correlated with the belief that life itself is the most precious possession? That a Christian wants life everlasting and afterlife is construed as like this life on earth? How can a faith be extenuated for a cause when a religion can only profess the lame reasoning of "the Lord works in mysterious ways that only He understands." And, "Ours is not the reason why, but have faith." In what? How can anyone with a sound reasoning mind have belief in a Creator who takes the life of a rare youth who is working for and living a life dedicated to that very Creator.

Is this Creator so cruel it should try and punish those who are not so dedicated? An all-loving God surely can't be so vindictive and blunt in his actions. Must faith in such a God be so blindly receptive to this being His will? That anyone questioning of His actions denounce unbelief?

Doesn't this mysterious way cause more rejection than acceptance? Can a father who loves his son with every ounce of feeling accept his death as being God's will without either a disbelief in there being a God at all or if there is, He is an unjust and unmerciful one. Wouldn't a person who accepts such a blow as "being the Lord's will" have to be an individualistic human whose sense of reasoning and thinking is limited to obeying and thinking anything he is told. How can meaningful belief be founded on nothing more than that you must accept everything unexplainable or unreasonable as being "a mysterious way of an all-knowing Lord." If "God so loved the world that He gave His only begotton son to perish," then how in the world could the same God do this to a father? Is the belief in this God formulated to cause fear or love? How can love culminate through such a tragedy if one truly believes that God is responsible for happiness.

REFLECTING ON DYING

This Sunday morning, July 6, 2014, I'm sitting in my teak deck chair on my redwood deck watching the finches 50 feet away from probably the most beautiful river in the world, with the gargling of rushing water over rocks and holes in a cacophony of a never-ending, soothing, sensual, subliminal sound as it makes it hurried rush to the ocean 150 miles away. Its noisy beginning here fades to a serene, placid flow of Willamette to Columbia to ocean on a 3-day journey. It will end in the tumultuous roar of the ocean, only to be picked up by the atmosphere in a non-ending cycle, depositing it in the mountains to begin it's recycling wonder only to flow past me again and again. Like life, it has its source, it has its flow, and it has its termination in the vast unknown. And it has its return to the source only to repeat another generation of force and wonder.

In watching these finches emptying their feeder, I'm sure they're not contemplating their own demise and the hereafter, or speculating on a God. Only enjoying the good fortune that finding a filled feeder and a life of pleasures; so should we all. This river doesn't run straight to its end. The journey has rocks, falls, holes, bends, and many miles of seemingly slow progress where the channel is wide and deep, but nevertheless, moving toward that ultimate ending which can't be seen but is inevitable. I was born and raised on that broad, swift flowing river and 85 years later, am living in serenity near the source. Heretofore was the rocks, the holes, the bends and the falls of that inevitable journey.

BATHROOM PHILOSOPHY

As I sat this morning on the throne waiting for the regular elimination of used body fuel and doing my heavy-duty thinking I noticed a black speck moving across the white vinyl floor indistinguishable as an ant or small termite. Although drifting in a bathtub direction he was going first one way then another, very evidently with no predetermined destination or goal in mind. So my analogy develops into our existence in this vast universe. First of all, how denigrating to not be recognized as either an ant or a termite. Second, being in the middle of this big world confused alone trying to figure out where to go, when actually he's on the bathroom floor. The to "nowhere" is as significant as a speck of dust as his journey only matters to him and that has no purpose. So is life, I suppose as viewed by greater source; God? Being one of six billion species of human life, is one more important than another? I didn't squash him since where he was going was not going to affect my life.

ROMANCE OF THE RIVER

I t only happens a few times, but when it does, the rapture—the feeling of total involvement in the pleasures of living—takes hold. Sitting on the deck on a still summer night, warm at eight, with just the sound of the river rushing over the rapids, can have the effect of the same thing as seeing Crater Lake for the first time, walking to the brim of the Grand Canyon, floating above the earth in a balloon. Your senses grasp the totality of it all. For some reason, more tonight than others. To experience this feeling alone is pure pleasure, to share with someone else, is overwhelming. Just sitting here, not talking, soaking up the sounds of the river and adding imagination to the surrounding quiet draws two souls together more connecting than any words. "Can I fix you a drink?" "No, I don't need one now." "How about a dessert?" "Thanks, but I am fine without one."

Quietly we sat here an hour with nothing but the romance of the river. Well, what about making love? With a nonchalance like accepting cream for her coffee, she said, "Yes, I could use some of the that," and gently takes my hand and enters the bedroom from the deck. "Leave the door open to hear the water." Tonight the romance of the river has enhanced the mood of our mutual feelings. Our act of making love has a depth of feeling, a sharing, an excitement, of a river rushing over rapids and then placidly moving through to the deep pools having expended his energy. In the tranquility of afterglow we hear the non-ending romance of this river.

It is said that flowing water has a calming and quieting effect. Such is the case tonight, sitting for an hour in my deck chair with only the sound of the river, seemed to tranquilize me with only my fantasies to enter my head. One thing is true, I need someone to share these moments with who has the same response that I do.

THE HIDDEN BOARD

How many times do I need to use something or some tool and I discover it's been discarded, lost, or just not findable? This morning I wanted to write and knew what I needed. Years ago, someone gave us a piece of plywood fashioned to rest on the arms of a chair, nicely finished, with a half-moon shape that made a perfect writing table. We remembered my mother using it, sitting in her old chair, writing and watching television. That's what I needed and mentioned this to my wife. "Well, I think that old writing board is in the back closet with the old movie projector and 2,000 feet of unedited film." Doubting her memory and her 100% sanity, I rummaged through that closet, and there standing in the back and covered up with my old corduroy coat I hadn't seen in 15 years was my mother's old board. I had salvaged it from mom's things, brought it home and promptly forgot it. I can brag one more time that my pack-rat philosophy of don't-throw-that-away-yet is vindicated, and I'm experiencing a nostalgic warmth of using the same old writing board of mom's, propped upon the arms in my rocker.

NEVER TAKE THE SAME ROAD HOME

"If a fork in the road, take it." - Yogi

Whenever we go on a trip it always seems to amaze my wife that I never like to take the same route home that I took getting to where we were going. When someone asks us how we are going to go home, why wife always says, "Well, I know it won't be the same way that we came because Dave will never take the same way home." Well that is probably a true statement and it holds true for many things that I've done in my life. I have never followed the outlined road that other people have taken and so I have made my own path and find that using different methods and ways of getting there is always more interesting.

In saying this, doing the same thing, the same way, every time, is a sure way to boredom. From where I live there are several different roads that go to town and the same thing is true in life. There are several different roads that lead to where you're going; maybe some longer than others but can offer a different view. There is nothing wrong with having a goal, but there can always be more than one way to reach it, so you don't need to follow the road that others have taken. The path selected may not be the best, but even GPS can get you lost, so the quickest and the shortest may not be the best. And, maybe the longer road can be the most adventurous. After all, the best life may not be the shortest from birth to death: it's the road you've taken that makes the difference.

BIRTHDAY REFLECTION

The old song says, "How nice it is to be loved by you." This old man truly enjoys, now more than before, those people who have made a special effort and recognition of his small desires to accommodate him on his birthday. Tonight I shall dine on petite oysters wrapped in thin bacon as hors d'oeuvres with superb dry raspberry wine. The only thing that could make it more enjoyable would be your company to make it extra special. Your presence, more than any presents, make my day and my life glow (now don't laugh, I am trying to be profound). Yesterday I noticed our old maple tree dropping its leaves and as Dyer would say, "From it's source," and, as life is, some leaves have already reached the end of their present life and are to their next destination while some are still green and have many more days to bask in the sun and feel the breeze. Yet, their destiny, is to separate from their source, fall to the ground, and return to their source. None have the power to determine when they shall go; that is determined by another power. This old leaf is experiencing that golden fall of life, and although not ready to fall yet, each birthday I fire my cannon (maybe only on the fourth of July), and continue to lead the parade. Come up soon and help finish the wine.

Love, Dave

EPILOGUE

The end hasn't been written and in fact all the events haven't been told. Each memory of living only enlivens ten more memories, so the whole story is never told. Telling of the events by Chip, being the youngest of the DeLapp family, does not touch the essence of each member; this is the tail wagging the dog. But my recollections are given life by my being the youngest and the focus of all my older brothers and sisters. It is my inheritance that writing and remembering has been left to me by my older brothers and sisters who have taken the course so often taken that, "maybe Chip will do it". So being the end of the line and 87 years old, Chip has finally done it. To relation and friends, I can only hope that it revives good memories. To those who aren't related or friends, I hope that to recall times and pleasures of other people has been interesting to you.

Chip